Collins
gem

Malay
phrasebook

Consultant

Marisa Amshah Mohd Isa

in association with First Edition Translations Ltd

First published 2008

Copyright © HarperCollins Publishers

Reprint 10 9 8 7 6 5 4 3 2 1 0

Typeset by Davidson Pre-Press, Glasgow

Printed in China through Golden Cup

Printing Services

www.collinslanguage.com

ISBN 13 978-0-00-727667-7

Using your phrasebook

Your *Collins Gem Phrasebook* is designed to help you locate the exact phrase you need, when you need it, whether on holiday or for business. If you want to adapt the phrases, you can easily see where to substitute your own words using the dictionary section, and the clear, full-colour layout gives you direct access to the different topics.

The Gem Phrasebook includes:

- Over 70 topics arranged thematically. Each phrase is accompanied by a simple pronunciation guide which eliminates any problems in pronouncing foreign words.

- A top ten tips section to safeguard against any cultural faux pas, giving essential dos and don'ts for situations involving local customs or etiquette.

- Practical hints to help make your stay trouble free, showing you where to go and what to do when dealing with everyday matters such as travel or hotels and offering valuable tourist information.

- Face-to-face sections so that you understand what it is being said to you. These example mini-dialogues give you a good idea of what to expect from a real conversation.

- Common announcements and messages you may hear, ensuring that you never miss the important information you need to know when out and about.

- A clearly laid-out dictionary which means you will never be stuck for words.

- A basic grammar section which will enable you to build on your phrases.

- A list of public holidays to avoid being caught out by unexpected opening and closing hours, and to make sure you don't miss the celebrations!

It's worth spending time before you embark on your travels just looking through the topics to see what is covered and becoming familiar with what might be said to you.

Whatever the situation, your *Gem Phrasebook* is sure to help!

Contents

5

Pronouncing Malay

••

Malay is a phonetic language, and has just a few simple consonant and vowel sounds which are easy to learn.

Vowels

Malay has 5 vowels: a, e, i, o, u.

The vowel 'e' can be pronounced two ways. The first sounds like the 'e' in 'red'. The second pronunciation (symbolized by ê in this phrasebook), has the schwa vowel sound, like the 'e' in 'vowel' or 'father'.

The vowel 'u' also has two slightly different sounds. The first sound is like the 'u' in 'lunar' and the second sound is like the shorter 'u' in 'pull'. The differences between the sounds are not indicated in written Malay, and you will learn to tell the difference as you learn more Malay words.

Unlike in English, there is no one stressed syllable in Malay words – each syllable is stressed equally.

Vowels	
a	as in **a**fter
ê (schwa)	as in vow**e**l
e	as in r**e**d
i	as in th**i**n
o	as in **o**ld
u	as in l**u**nar
u	as in p**u**ll

Consonants

Malay consonant sounds are similar to the English consonant sounds. The exceptions are the sounds for 'c', 'kh' and 'sy' as listed below.

b	= as in **b**lue
c	= like ch as in **ch**ange
d	= as in **d**og
f	= as in **f**lame
g	= as in **g**reen
h	= as in **h**and (aspirated)
j	= like dg as in ba**dg**e
k	= like c as in **c**ap (silent when it appears at the end of a word)
kh	= like ch as in the Scottish 'lo**ch**' or German 'i**ch**'
l	= as in **l**ike
m	= as in **m**other

n	= as in **n**ight
p	= as in **p**late
q	= as in **q**uestion
r	= like rr as in the Spanish ce**rr**o (silent when it appears at the end of a word)
s	= as in **s**ave
sy	= like sh as in **sh**ut
t	= as in **t**ool
v	= as in **v**ain
w	= as in **w**ait
x	= like cks as in bri**cks**
y	= as in **y**ellow
z	= like z as in ra**z**or

The following are a few sounds that may be a little tricky to pronounce:

ny	= like ny as in ca**ny**on
ng	= like ng as in si**ng**
ngg	= like the hard-sounding ng as in li**ng**o

Common dipthongs

au	= like 'ow' as in h**ow**
ai	= like 'i' as in d**i**ne
oi	= like 'oy' as in t**oy**

Top ten tips

1 Look out for the Malaysian Tourist Police on patrol at tourist spots if you need help. They wear dark blue shirts and trousers, chequered hatbands and a badge with the letter 'I' (for 'Information') on their chests.

2 Malaysia is a multireligious country, but the official religion is Islam. Dress and behave respectfully in public, particularly in non-urban areas.

3 Muslims do not drink alcohol and eat only halal meat (animals slaughtered and processed according to Muslim law). Try to refrain from eating or drinking in front of Muslims when they are fasting during Ramadan. The Muslim call to prayer occurs five times a day – it is considered extremely rude to criticize or complain about it.

4 You can greet Malaysians by gently shaking their right hands and then momentarily placing your hand on your heart as a sign of sincerity. Do not offer your hand to Muslim women. Instead, greet them by smiling and nodding your head to them.

5   You should address Malaysians by their first name and add the word '**Encik**' (for men) or '**Cik**' or '**Puan**' (for women) before it. You can also use '**Pakcik**' (for older men) or '**Makcik**' (for older women).

6   Public displays of intimacy between couples, particularly same-sex couples, are discouraged.

7   When visiting Malaysians in their homes, it is polite to bring a small gift, such as fruit. If the host offers you some refreshment, it is impolite to refuse.

8   Use your right hand when handling food, and for giving or receiving something. It is normal for Malaysians to eat with their right hands at home or in restaurants.

9   When pointing, do so with your right thumb and not your finger or foot. Beckon someone over by wiggling your fingers with your whole palm facing downwards.

10 Be prepared to remove your shoes before entering homes or places of worship.

Talking to people

Hello/goodbye, yes/no

• •

Common Malay greetings are easy to remember because the word '**Selamat**' (literally meaning 'safe') is used frequently. For example, '**Selamat pagi**' is 'good morning', '**Selamat petang**' is 'good evening', '**Selamat maju jaya**' is 'all the best', '**Selamat datang**' is 'welcome', and so on.

Goodbye	**Selamat jalan**
	sê-la-mat ja-lan
Farewell	**Selamat tinggal**
	sê-la-mat teeng-gal
See you again	**Jumpa lagi**
	joom-pa la-gee
See you tomorrow	**Jumpa lagi esok**
	joom-pa la-gee eh-sok
Yes	**Ya**
	ya
No	**Tidak**
	tee-dak

Please	**Tolong**
	toh-long
Thank you/	**Terima kasih**
Thanks	tê-ree-ma ka-sih
Sorry!	**Maaf!**
	ma-af!
Excuse me!	**Maafkan saya!** *or*
(before a question)	**Tumpang tanya!**
	ma-af-kan sa-ya *or*
	toom-pang ta-nya
I don't	**Saya tak faham**
understand	sa-ya tak fa-ham
I cannot speak	**Saya tidak boleh bertutur**
Malay	**dalam bahasa Melayu**
	sa-ya tee-dak bo-leh bêr-too-toor
	da-lam ba-ha-sa mê-la-yoo

Key phrases

· ·

Where is...?	**Di manakah...?**
	dee ma-na-kah...?
Where is the	**Di manakah bank yang**
nearest bank?	**terdekat?**
	dee ma-na-kah benk yang
	têr-dê-kat?
Where is the	**Di manakah tandas?**
toilet?	dee ma-na-kah tan-das?

How...?	**Bagaimana...?** ba-gai-ma-na...?
How much does it cost?	**Berapa harganya?** bê-ra-pa har-ga-nia?
Is it included...?	**Adakah termasuk...?** ah-da-kah têr-ma-suk...?
When is/are...?	**Bilakah...?** bee-la-kah...?
When is breakfast?	**Bilakah sarapan pagi?** bee-la-kah sa-ra-pan pa-gee?
When are we going?	**Bila kita nak pergi?** bee-la kee-ta nak pêr-gee?
What time is it?	**Pukul berapa sekarang?** poo-kul bê-ra-pa sê-ka-rang?
At what time...?	**Pada pukul berapa...?** pa-da poo-kul bê-ra-pa...?
What is it?	**Ada apa?** ah-da ah-pa?
Which one?	**Yang mana satu?** yang ma-na sa-too?
Why? (there is no difference between these two words – each can be used in all circumstances)	**Kenapa/Mengapa?** kê-na-pa/mê-nga-pa?

Why do you do this?	**Kenapa/Mengapa anda lakukan ini?**
	kê-na-pa/mê-nga-pa an-da la-koo-kan ee-nee?
Please leave!	**Sila pergi!**
	see-la pêr-gee!
Do you have...?	**Anda ada...?**
	an-da ah-da...?
Do you have some stamps?	**Anda ada setem?**
	an-da ah-da sê-tem?
Do you have a map?	**Anda ada peta?**
	an-da ah-da pê-ta?
I would like...	**Saya mahu...**
	sa-ya ma-hoo...
I would like a cup of water	**Saya mahu secawan air**
	sa-ya ma-hoo sê-cha-wan a-yer
I would like a bottle of beer	**Saya mahu sebotol bir**
	sa-ya ma-hoo sê-bo-tol bir
Can I...?	**Bolehkah saya...?**
	bo-leh-kah sa-ya...?
Can I use your phone?	**Bolehkah saya guna telefon anda?**
	bo-leh-kah sa-ya goo-na teh-lee-fon an-da?
Can I smoke?	**Bolehkan saya merokok?**
	bo-leh-kah sa-ya mê-ro-kok?
There is/are...	**Ada...**
	ah-da...

There is a fitness centre in this hotel	**Ada pusat kesihatan di dalam hotel ini**
	ah-da poo-sat kê-see-ha-tan dee da-lam ho-tel ee-nee
There isn't...	**Tidak ada...**
	tee-dak ah-da...
There isn't a room available	**Tidak ada bilik kosong**
	tee-dak ah-da bee-lek ko-song

Signs and notices

• •

buka	boo-ka	open
tutup	too-tup	closed
Wanita	wa-nee-ta	Ladies
Lelaki	lê-la-kee	Gentlemen
layan-diri	la-yan-dee-ree	self-service
tolak	to-lak	push
tarik	ta-rik	pull
meja tunai	me-ja too-nai	cash desk
air minuman	ah-yer mee-noo-man	drinking water
tandas	tan-das	toilets
kosong	ko-song	vacant
sibuk	see-buk	engaged
bilik kecemasan	bee-lek kê-chê-ma-san	emergency room

bantuan kecemasan	ban-too-wan kê-chê-ma-san	first aid
penuh	pê-nuh	full
berhenti	bêr-hên-tee	stop
rosak	ro-sak	out of order
untuk disewa	oon-tuk dee-seh-wa	for rent
untuk dijual	oon-tuk dee-joo-wal	for sale
jualan	joo-wa-lan	sales
bawah tanah	ba-wah ta-nah	basement
tingkat bawah	ting-kat ba-wah	ground floor
masuk	ma-suk	entrance
pejabat tiket	pê-ja-bat tee-ket	ticket office
balai polis	ba-lai po-lis	police station
barang hilang	ba-rang hee-lang	lost property
berlepas	bêr-lê-pas	departures
ketibaan	kê-tee-ba-an	arrivals
dilarang	dee-la-rang	prohibited
simpan bagasi	sim-pan ba-ga-see	left luggage
persendirian	pêr-sên-dee-ree-yan	private
panas	pa-nas	hot
sejuk	se-juk	cold
bahaya	ba-ha-ya	danger
dilarang merokok	dee-la-rang mê-ro-kok	no smoking

17

jangan sentuh	ja-ngan sên-tuh	do not touch
keluar	kê-loo-war	exit
bilik salinan	bee-lik sa-lee-nan	changing room
bilik air	bee-lik ah-yer	bathroom
hati-hati	ha-tee-ha-tee	caution
maklumat	mak-loo-mat	information
pertanyaan	pêr-ta-nia-an	enquiries

Polite expressions

• •

Malaysians are generally a friendly lot, and most will do their best to help tourists in need. Some may be a little shy at first and may avoid direct eye-contact when first approached. Be sure to approach them humbly with a smile and say something as simple as '**helo**' ('hello'). Below are some common phrases you will hear and use:

How do you do?	**Apa khabar?**
	ah-pa kha-bar?
I am fine	**Saya sihat**
	sa-ya see-hat
Thank you	**Terima kasih**
	tê-ree-ma ka-sih
My name is...	**Nama saya...**
	na-ma sa-ya...

Welcome!	**Selamat Datang!**
	sê-la-mat da-tang!
Yes, Sir	**Ya, Tuan**
	ya, too-wan
Pardon me/	**Maafkan saya** or
Excuse me	**Tumpang tanya**
	ma-af-kan sa-ya or
	toom-pang ta-nya
This is...	**Ini...**
	ee-nee...
This is my	**Ini suami saya**
husband	ee-nee soo-wa-mee sa-ya
This is my wife	**Ini isteri saya**
	ee-nee is-tê-ri sa-ya
Enjoy your meal!	**Nikmati hidangan anda!**
	neek-ma-tee hee-da-ngan an-da!
Pleased to	**Gembira bertemu anda**
meet you	gêm-bee-ra bêr-tê-moo an-da
The meal was	**Sedapnya hidangan tadi**
delicious	sê-dap-nia hee-da-ngan ta-dee
Thank you	**Terima kasih banyak-banyak**
very much	tê-ree-ma ka-sih ba-niak ba-niak
Have a good trip!	**Selamat jalan!**
	sê-la-mat ja-lan!
Enjoy your	**Nikmati percutian anda!**
holiday!	neek-ma-tee pêr-choo-tee-yan
	an-da!

Celebrations

• •

Happy birthday!	**Selamat hari jadi!**
	sê-la-mat ha-ree ja-dee!
Congratulations!	**Tahniah!**
	tah-nee-yah!
Cheers!	**Selamat!**
(only as a toast)	sê-la-mat!
Happy New Year!	**Selamat Tahun Baru!**
	sê-la-mat ta-hun ba-roo!

Making friends

• •

Hello my name is...	**Helo nama saya...**
	he-lo na-ma sa-ya...
What is your name?	**Apa nama anda?**
	ah-pa na-ma an-da?
Where are you from?	**Anda berasal dari mana?**
	an-da bêr-ah-sal da-ree ma-na?
I am from England	**Saya berasal dari England**
	sa-ya bêr-ah-sal da-ree ing-lên
Nice to meet you	**Gembira bertemu anda**
	gêm-bee-ra bêr-tê-moo an-da
How old are you?	**Berapa umur anda?**
	bê-ra-pa oo-moor an-da?

> **Public holidays** (p 157)

I'm ... years old	**Saya berumur ... tahun**	
	sa-ya bêr-oo-moor ... ta-hoon	
Where do you live?	**Anda tinggal di mana?**	
	an-da teeng-gal dee ma-na?	
I live in London	**Saya tinggal di London**	
	sa-ya teeng-gal dee lan-dên	
Are you married?	**Anda sudah berkahwin?**	
	an-da soo-dah bêr-kah-win?	
Do you have any children?	**Anda ada anak?**	
	an-da ah-da ah-nak?	
I have children	**Saya ada anak**	
	sa-ya ah-da ah-nak	
I don't have children	**Saya tidak ada anak**	
	sa-ya tee-dak ah-da ah-nak	
I have a boyfriend/ girlfriend	**Saya ada teman lelaki/ teman wanita**	
	sa-ya ah-da tê-man lê-la-ki/ tê-man wa-ni-ta	
I'm single	**Saya bujang**	
	sa-ya boo-jang	
I'm married	**Saya sudah berkahwin**	
	sa-ya soo-dah bêr-kah-win	
I'm divorced	**Saya sudah bercerai**	
	sa-ya soo-dah bêr-chê-rai	

Making friends

> **Work** (p 22) > **Leisure/beach** (p 78)

Work

What is your job?	**Apa pekerjaan anda?**
	ah-pa pê-kêr-ja-an an-da?
Do you enjoy it?	**Anda suka?**
	an-da soo-ka?
I'm a doctor	**Saya doktor**
	sa-ya dok-tor
I'm a teacher	**Saya cikgu**
	sa-ya chik-goo
I'm a nurse	**Saya jururawat**
	sa-ya joo-roo-ra-wat
I work in a shop	**Saya bekerja di sebuah kedai**
	sa-ya bê-kêr-ja dee sê-boo-wah kê-dai
I work in a factory	**Saya bekerja di sebuah kilang**
	sa-ya bê-kêr-ja dee sê-boo-wah kee-lang
I work in a bank	**Saya bekerja di sebuah bank**
	sa-ya bê-kêr-ja dee sê-boo-wah benk
I work from home	**Saya bekerja dari rumah**
	sa-ya bê-kêr-ja da-ree roo-mah

> **Making friends** (p 20)

Weather

••

cerah	chê-rah	clear
hujan	hoo-jan	rainy
sejuk	sê-juk	cold
panas	pa-nas	hot
bermatahari		sunny
bêr-ma-ta-ha-ree		
berangin	bêr-ah-ngin	windy
ramalan cuaca		weather forecast
ra-ma-lan choo-wa-cha		

It's sunny	**Cuaca bermatahari**
	choo-wa-cha bêr-ma-ta-ha-ree
It's raining	**Cuaca hujan**
	choo-wa-cha hoo-jan
It's windy	**Cuaca berangin**
	choo-wa-cha bêr-ah-ngin
It's very hot	**Cuaca sangat panas**
	choo-wa-cha sa-ngat pa-nas
What is the temperature?	**Berapa suhu sekarang?**
	bê-ra-pa soo-hoo sê-ka-rang?
What is the weather forecast for tomorrow?	**Apakah ramalan cuaca untuk esok?**
	ah-pa-kah ra-ma-lan choo-wa-cha oon-tuk eh-sok?

Does it get cool at night?	**Adakah cuaca lebih sejuk pada waktu malam?**
	ah-da-kah choo-wa-cha lê-bih sê-juk pa-da wak-too ma-lam?
Will there be a storm?	**Nak ribut kah?**
	nak ree-but kah?
What beautiful weather!	**Cuaca sangat indah!**
	choo-wa-cha sa-ngat in-dah!
What awful weather!	**Cuaca sangat teruk!**
	choo-wa-cha sa-ngat tê-ruk!

Getting around

Asking the way

kiri kee-ree	left
kanan ka-nan	right
jalan terus ja-lan tê-roos	straight on
bertentangan dengan bêr-tên-ta-ngan dê-ngan	opposite
di sebelah dee sê-bê-lah	next to
lampu trafik lam-poo tra-fik	traffic lights
di selekoh dee sê-le-koh	at the corner

FACE TO FACE

A **Tumpang tanya. Di manakah pejabat pos?**
toom-pang ta-nya. dee ma-na-kah pê-ja-bat pos?
Excuse me. Where is the post office?

B **Jalan terus dan belok kanan/kiri di selekoh**
ja-lan tê-roos dan be-lok ka-nan/kee-ree dee
sê-le-koh
Keep straight on and turn right/left at the corner

25

A **Jauhkah?**
ja-wuh-kah?
Is it far?

B **Tidak. Cuma 200 meter/2 minit dari sini**
tee-dak. choo-ma 200 me-têr/2 mi-nit da-ree see-nee
No. Only 200 metres/2 minutes away

A **Terima kasih**
tê-ree-ma ka-sih
Thank you

B **Sama-sama**
sa-ma-sa-ma
You are welcome

Where is...?	**Di manakah...?**
	dee ma-na-kah...?
Where is the	**Di manakah muzium?**
museum?	dee ma-na-kah moo-zi-yoom?
How do I get...?	**Bagaimana cara untuk pergi ke...?**
	ba-gai-ma-na cha-ra oon-tuk pêr-gee kê...?
How do I get to	**Bagaimana cara untuk pergi ke muzeum?**
the museum?	ba-gai-ma-na cha-ra oon-tuk pêr-gee kê moo-zee-yoom?
to the coach station	**ke stesen bas**
	kê steh-sen bas

to the beach	**ke pantai**
	kê pan-tai
to my hotel	**ke hotel saya**
	kê ho-tel sa-ya

YOU MAY HEAR...	
Belok kiri	Turn left
be-lok kee-ree	
Belok kanan	Turn right
be-lok ka-nan	
Jalan terus	Keep straight on
ja-lan tê-roos	
Lebih dekat dengan	Closer to
lê-bih dê-kat dê-ngan	

Bus and coach

• •

Most cities and towns in Malaysia have public bus services run by several small companies. KL Sentral is the main hub of the transportation system in Kuala Lumpur. Within Kuala Lumpur and the Klang Valley, Rapid KL buses cover over 100 routes and charge very affordable prices for all-day, unlimited

> **Maps and guides** (p 70)

ride tickets. There are four main bus stations in Kuala Lumpur:

Puduraya Bus Terminal, which is the main station for buses to and from all parts of Malaysia and also Singapore.

Hentian Putra, which has express coach services to the east coast of Malaysia.

Hentian Duta, where you will find mainly north-bound buses.

Pekeliling Bus Terminal, with buses mainly heading out to the eastern states.

Coach tickets sell out quickly during the school holidays and festive seasons. Booking in advance is highly recommended.

perhentian bas pêr-hên-tee-yan bas	bus stop
stesen bas steh-sen bas	coach station
tiket tee-ket	ticket

FACE TO FACE

A Tumpang tanya. Yang mana satukah bas pukul sepuluh ke Melaka?
toom-pang ta-nya. yang ma-na sa-too-kah bas poo-kul sê-poo-luh kê mê-la-ka?
Excuse me. Which one is the 10 o'clock Malacca bus?

B **Yang di sebelah kanan/kiri. Bas biru.**
yang dee sê-bê-lah kah-nan/kee-ree. bas bee-roo.
The one on the right/left. The blue bus.

Where is the coach station?	**Di manakah stesen bas?** dee ma-na-kah steh-sen bas?
I am going to...	**Saya dalam perjalanan ke...** sa-ya da-lam pêr-ja-la-nan kê...
Is there a bus to...?	**Ada tak bas yang pergi ke...?** ah-da tak bas yang pêr-gee kê...?
Does it go to...?	**Adakah ia pergi ke...?** ah-da-kah ee-ya pêr-gee kê...?
It goes to...	**Ia pergi ke...** ee-ya pêr-gee kê...
to the airport	**ke lapangan terbang** kê la-pa-ngan têr-bang
to the beach	**ke pantai** kê pan-tai
to the shopping centre	**ke pusat membeli-belah** kê poo-sat mêm-bê-lee-bê-lah
1 ticket	**1 tiket** 1 tee-ket
2 tickets	**2 tiket** 2 tee-ket
3 tickets	**3 tiket** 3 tee-ket
When is the next bus?	**Bilakah bas seterusnya?** bee-la-kah bas sê-tê-roos-nia?

Tidak ada bas tee-dak ah-da bas	There is no bus
Anda mesti naik teksi an-da mês-ti na-yek tek-see	You must take a taxi
Tiket sudah habis tee-ket soo-dah ha-bis	The tickets are sold out

Metro/LRT (light rail transit)

• •

This is a convenient and quick way to travel across
Kuala Lumpur and the surrounding suburbs in the
Klang Valley. The Kelana Jaya Line (KLJ) and Ampang
Rail Line (AMP) are both run by Rapid KL. Their
hours of operation are from 6 am to after 11 pm
daily. Tickets can be bought at all Rapid KL Rail
stations and bus terminals. PUTRA-LRT also
operates buses to shuttle passengers to and fro
within a 3-kilometre radius of each LRT station.
Each trip costs RM0.50.

| **Masuk** ma-suk | Entrance |
| **Jalan keluar**
ja-lan kê-loo-war | Way out |

> **Luggage** (p 99)

Where is the nearest metro station?	**Di manakah stesen LRT yang terdekat?**
	dee ma-na-kah steh-sen el-ar-tee yang têr-dê-kat?
How does the ticket machine work?	**Bagaimana mesin tiket ini berfungsi?**
	ba-gai-ma-na meh-sin tee-ket ee-nee bêr-foong-see?
Do you have a map of the metro?	**Anda ada peta stesen LRT?**
	an-da ah-da pê-ta steh-sen el-ar-tee?
I'm going to...	**Saya hendak ke...**
	sa-ya hên-dak kê...
How do I get to...?	**Bagaimana cara untuk saya pergi ke...?**
	ba-gai-ma-na cha-ra oon-tuk sa-ya pêr-gee kê...?
How do we get to...?	**Bagaimana cara untuk kami pergi ke...?**
	ba-gai-ma-na cha-ra oon-tuk ka-mee pêr-gee kê...?
Do I have to change trains?	**Perlukah saya bertukar keretapi?**
	pêr-loo-kah sa-ya bêr-too-kar kê-re-ta-pee?
What is the next stop?	**Apakah perhentian seterusnya?**
	ah-pa-kah pêr-hên-tee-yan sê-têr-roos-nia?

Metro/LRT

Excuse me. I'm getting off here	**Maafkan saya. Saya hendak turun di sini**
	ma-afkan saya. sa-ya hên-dak too-roon dee see-nee
Please let me through	**Tumpang lalu**
	toom-pang la-loo

Train

• •

Keretapi Tanah Melayu Berhad (KTMB) offers affordable services in Peninsular Malaysia. Its western line runs from Thailand to Singapore, while the eastern line covers certain areas on the East Coast. Fare prices depend on destination and whether you want to travel by first, second or third class. KTMB also has sleeper trains for overnight journeys. Foreign tourists can purchase KTM rail passes, which allow unlimited travel on intercity trains and are valid from 5 to 15 days. KTMB tickets are available at all KTMB stations or via the Internet at **www.ktmb.com.my**.

> **Luggage** (p 99)

stesen steh-sen	station
keretapi kê-re-ta-pee	train
platform plat-form	platform
tempat duduk têm-pat doo-duk	seat
tiket tee-ket	ticket
pejabat tempahan pê-ja-bat têm-pa-han	booking office
jadual ja-doo-wal	timetable
penyambung pê-nyam-boong	connection

FACE TO FACE

A **Bilakah keretapi seterusnya ke Seremban?**
bee-la-kah kê-re-ta-pee sê-tê-roos-nia kê sê-rêm-ban?
When is the next train to Seremban?

B **Pada pukul sepuluh**
pa-da poo-kul sê-poo-luh
At 10 o'clock

3 tickets please	**Tolong berikan saya tiga tiket** toh-long bê-ree-kan sa-ya tee-ga tee-ket
Single or return?	**Satu atau dua hala?** sa-too ah-tau doo-wa ha-la?

33

Return, please	**Tolong berikan saya tiket dua hala** toh-long bê-ree-kan sa-ya tee-ket doo-wa ha-la
Where is the station?	**Di manakah stesen?** dee ma-na-kah steh-sen?
a single	**satu tiket sehala** sa-too tee-ket sê-ha-la
2 singles	**Dua tiket sehala** doo-wa tee-ket sê-ha-la
a single to Kuantan	**satu tiket sehala ke Kuantan** sa-too tee-ket sê-ha-la kê koo-wan-tan
2 singles to Johor Bahru	**dua tiket sehala ke Johor Bahru** doo-wa tee-ket sê-ha-la kê jo-hor bah-roo
a return	**satu tiket dua hala** sa-too tee-ket doo-wa ha-la
2 returns	**dua tiket dua hala** doo-wa tee-ket doo-wa ha-la
1 adult	**satu dewasa** sa-too de-wa-sa
2 children	**dua kanak-kanak** doo-wa ka-nak-ka-nak
2 adults	**dua dewasa** doo-wa de-wa-sa
first class	**kelas pertama** kê-las pêr-ta-ma

second class	**kelas kedua**
	kê-las kê-doo-wa
smoking	**merokok**
	mê-ro-kok
non-smoking	**dilarang merokok**
	dee-la-rang mê-ro-kok
I want to book a seat	**Saya hendak tempah tempat duduk**
	sa-ya hên-dak têm-pah têm-pat doo-duk
Which platform?	**Platform yang mana?**
	plat-form yang ma-na?
When does it get to Alor Setar?	**Bila ia akan sampai di Alor Setar?**
	bee-la ee-ya ah-kan sam-pai di ah-lor star?
When does it leave?	**Bilakah ia akan berlepas?**
	bee-la-kah ee-ya ah-kan bêr-lê-pas?
When does it arrive?	**Bilakah ia akan tiba?**
	bee-la-kah ee-ya ah-kan tee-ba?
Is this seat free?	**Adakah tempat duduk ini kosong?**
	ah-da-kah têm-pat doo-duk ee-nee ko-song?
Excuse me!	**Maafkan saya!**
	ma-af-kan sa-ya!

Train

> **Luggage** (p 99)

Taxi

You will find registered taxi services easily at airports, hotels, railway stations and bus stations. You can also telephone a taxi company or hail a cab from the street. Taxis in Kuala Lumpur and surrounding areas are metered, while taxi stands at the Kuala Lumpur International Airport (KLIA) and KL Sentral use a pre-paid coupon system. Beware of unauthorized taxi services at KLIA. To avoid being overcharged by unscrupulous taxi drivers, insist that the meter be turned on. If using an unmetered taxi outside the city, be sure to negotiate the price in advance.

Where can I get a taxi?	**Di mana boleh saya dapatkan teksi?**
	dee ma-na bo-leh sa-ya da-pat-kan tek-see?
I want to go to...	**Saya hendak pergi ke...**
	sa-ya hên-dak pêr-gee kê...
How much is it?	**Berapa harganya?**
	bê-ra-pa har-ga-nia?
To the airport, please	**Tolong pergi ke lapangan terbang**
	toh-long pêr-gee kê la-pa-ngan têr-bang
To the beach, please	**Tolong pergi ke pantai**
	toh-long pêr-gee kê pan-tai

36

Please stop here	**Sila berhenti di sini**	
	see-la bêr-hên-tee dee see-nee	
Please wait	**Sila tunggu**	
	see-la toong-goo	
It's too expensive	**Ia terlalu mahal**	
	ee-ya têr-la-loo ma-hal	
I haven't got any change	**Saya tidak ada duit kecik**	
	sa-ya tee-dak ah-da doo-wit kê-chik	
Keep the change	**Simpan bakinya**	
	seem-pan ba-ki-nia	

Boat

Malaysia has several beautiful islands which are perfect getaways from the busy cities. Most of the major islands like Pulau Redang, Pulau Perhentian and Pulau Tioman offer tourists the chance to travel by boat or ferry to and from the mainland. You can also enjoy cruising on rivers and lakes at places like Taman Negara. In the East Malaysian states of Sabah and Sarawak, the use of air-conditioned express boats and small river craft is common; especially in more rural areas. Call a local tour agent for details of boat services to the location you have in mind.

> **Luggage** (p 99)

37

pejabat tiket pê-ja-bat tee-ket	ticket office
jadual ja-doo-wal	timetable
ketibaan kê-tee-ba-an	arrival
berlepas bêr-lê-pas	departure

When is the next boat?	**Bilakah bot seterusnya?** bee-la-kah bot sê-tê-roos-nia?
When is the last boat?	**Bilakah bot terakhir?** bee-la-kah bot têr-a-khir?
We want to go to...	**Kami hendak pergi ke...** ka-mee hên-dak pêr-gee kê...
Is there a timetable?	**Ada tak jadual waktu?** ah-da tak ja-doo-wal waktu?
When does the boat leave?	**Bilakah bot akan berlepas?** bee-la-kah bot akan bêr-lê-pas?
How long does it take?	**Berapa lama perjalanannya?** bê-ra-pa la-ma pêr-ja-la-nan-nia?

Air travel

....

lapangan terbang la-pa-ngan têr-bang	airport
get get	gate
ketibaan kê-tee-ba-an	arrivals
berlepas bêr-lê-pas	departures
penerbangan pê-nêr-ba-ngan	flight
domestik do-mes-tik	domestic
antarabangsa an-ta-ra-bang-sa	international
maklumat mak-loo-mat	information

To the airport, please	**Tolong pergi ke lapangan terbang** to-long pêr-gee kê la-pa-ngan têr-bang
My flight is at one o'clock	**Penerbangan saya ialah pada pukul satu** pê-nêr-ba-ngan sa-ya ee-ya-lah pa-da poo-kul sa-too
How much is it to the airport?	**Berapa harganya untuk pergi ke lapangan terbang?** bê-ra-pa har-ga-nia oon-tuk pêr-gee kê la-pa-ngan têr-bang?

> **Emergencies** (p 106)

39

How much is it to the town centre?	**Berapa harganya untuk pergi ke pusat bandar?**
	bê-ra-pa har-ga-nia oon-tuk pêr-gee kê poo-sat ban-dar?
When will the flight leave?	**Penerbangan akan berlepas pada pukul berapa?**
	pê-nêr-ba-ngan ah-kan bêr-lê-pas pa-da poo-kul bê-ra-pa?

YOU MAY HEAR...

| **Pergi ke get nombor...** | Go to gate number... |
| pêr-gee kê get nom-bor... | |

Customs control

. . . .

Malaysia enforces very strict drug laws. A mandatory
death penalty awaits convicted drug traffickers.
If you bring in taxable items, you may have to pay
a refundable deposit for temporary importation.
Be sure you carry proof of purchase for the items,
and ask the customs officer for a receipt if you are
made to pay duty or a deposit. Goods such as
cosmetics, cameras and watches are duty-free.

> **Luggage** (p 99)

pasport pas-port		passport
kastam kas-tam		customs
arak ah-rak		alcohol
tembakau têm-ba-kau		tobacco

Do I have to pay duty on this?	**Haruskah saya bayar cukai untuk ini?**
	ha-roos-kah sa-ya ba-yar choo-kai oon-tuk ee-nee?
It is my medicine	**Ini ubat saya**
	ee-nee oo-bat sa-ya
The children are on this passport	**Anak-anak ada di dalam pasport ini**
	ah-nak-ah-nak ah-da dee da-lam pas-port ee-nee
I bought this duty-free	**Saya beli ini bebas cukai**
	sa-ya bê-lee ee-nee be-bas choo-kai

Driving

Car hire

....

To rent a vehicle, you need to have a valid driver's licence or, better still, an International Driving Licence. You must be between 23 years and 65 years of age and have at least one year's driving experience. You will find many international and local car rental companies in the big cities, especially at places like the larger airports, hotels and railway stations.

dokumen insuran do-koo-mên in-soo-ran	insurance documents
lesen memandu leh-sen mê-man-doo	driving licence

I want to hire a car	**Saya hendak sewa kereta** sa-ya hên-dak seh-wa kê-re-ta
with automatic gears	**dengan gear automatik** dê-ngan gee-yar oh-toh-ma-tik

for 1 day	**untuk satu hari**
	oon-tuk sa-too ha-ree
for 2 days	**untuk dua hari**
	oon-tuk doo-wa ha-ree
How much is it?	**Berapa harganya?**
	bê-ra-pa har-ga-nia?
Is insurance included?	**Termasuk insuran?**
	têr-ma-suk in-soo-ran?
Is there a deposit to pay?	**Perlu bayar deposit?**
	pêr-loo ba-yar dee-po-sit?
Can I pay by credit card?	**Boleh saya bayar dengan kad kredit?**
	bo-leh sa-ya ba-yar dê-ngan kad kreh-dit?
What petrol does it take?	**Ia guna petrol jenis apa?**
	ee-ya goo-na peh-trol jê-nis ah-pa?

Driving

Driving is done on the left-hand side of the road. Navigating traffic in Kuala Lumpur can be very challenging, especially during peak hours when there is a rush into or out of the city. Car parks are sometimes limited, especially in the heart of the city. Seatbelts are a must and the use of mobile phones while driving is forbidden.

hati-hati/bahaya ha-tee-ha-tee/ba-ha-ya	caution/danger
berhenti bêr-hên-tee	stop
lebuh raya lê-buh ra-ya	motorway
pusat bandar poo-sat ban-dar	town centre

Can I park here?	**Bolehkah saya letak kereta di sini?** bo-leh-kah sa-ya lê-tak kê-re-ta dee-see-nee?
How long can I park for?	**Berapa lama boleh saya letak kereta?** bê-ra-pa la-ma bo-leh sa-ya lê-tak kê-re-ta?
We are driving to...	**Kami sedang memandu ke...** ka-mee sê-dang mê-man-doo kê...
Is the road good?	**Adakah jalannya bagus?** ah-da-kah ja-lan-nia ba-goos?
How long will it take?	**Berapa lama perjalanannya?** bê-ra-pa la-ma pêr-ja-la-nan-nia?

YOU MAY HEAR...

Anda memandu terlalu laju an-da mê-man-doo têr-la-loo la-joo	You are driving too fast

Sila tunjukkan lesen memandu anda	Your driving licence, please
see-la toon-juk-kan leh-sen mê-man-doo an-da	

Petrol

• •

Petrol and diesel are widely available at petrol stations located throughout the country. Some petrol stations are open 24 hours, and most have a small shop that sells a variety of products like refreshments, souvenirs and the local newspapers.

petrol peh-trol	petrol
petrol tanpa plumbum peh-trol tan-pa ploom-boom	unleaded petrol
disel dee-sel	diesel

Where is the nearest petrol station?	**Di manakah stesen petrol yang terdekat?**
	dee-ma-na-kah steh-sen peh-trol yang têr-dê-kat?

Fill it up, please	**Tolong isi sampai penuh**
	toh-long ee-see sam-pai pê-nuh
Please check the oil	**Tolong periksa minyak**
	toh-long pê-rik-sa mee-niak
Can I pay by credit card?	**Boleh saya bayar dengan kad kredit?**
	bo-leh sa-ya ba-yar dê-ngan kad kreh-dit?

YOU MAY HEAR...	
Kami tidak ada... ka-mee tee-dak ah-da...	We have no...
Anda perlukan minyak an-da pêr-loo-kan mee-niak	You need oil
Anda perlukan air an-da pêr-loo-kan ah-yer	You need water
Anda perlukan angin an-da pêr-loo-kan ah-ngin	You need air

Driving

Breakdown

• •

A 24-hour emergency breakdown assistance service
is provided by the Automobile Association of
Malaysia (AAM). They can be reached at 1-800-880-
808. If your car breaks down on the North South
Expressway (which runs the length of Peninsular
Malaysia), use the emergency phones that can be
found every 2 kilometres. The highway company
(PLUS) operates a 24-hour emergency service and
has mechanics to attend to minor problems free of
charge. They will also tow your vehicle to the
nearest garage (repair shop) for further assistance
if necessary.

My car has broken down	**Kereta saya rosak** kê-re-ta sa-ya ro-sak
Can you help me?	**Boleh anda bantu saya?** bo-leh an-da ban-too sa-ya?
I've run out of petrol	**Saya kehabisan minyak** sa-ya kê-ha-bi-san mee-niak
I have a flat tyre	**Tayar saya pancit** ta-yar sa-ya pan-chit
Where is the nearest garage? (repair shop)	**Di manakah woksyop yang terdekat?** dee ma-na-kah work-shop yang têr-dê-kat?

Can you repair it?	**Anda boleh baiki?**
	an-da bo-leh bai-kee?
How long will it take?	**Berapa lama?**
	bê-ra-pa la-ma?
How much will it cost?	**Berapa harganya?**
	bê-ra-pa har-ga-nia?

Car parts

... doesn't work	**... tidak berfungsi**
	... tee-dak bêr-foong-see
Where is the garage? (repair shop)	**Di manakah kedai baiki?**
	dee ma-na-kah kê-dai bai-kee?

accelerator	pemecut	pê-mê-choot
alternator	pengulang alik	pêng-oo-lang ah-lik
battery	bateri	ba-tê-ree
brakes	brek	brek
choke	cok	chok
clutch	cekam	chê-kam
engine	enjin	en-jin
exhaust pipe	paip ekzos	pa-yip ek-zos
fuse	fius	fi-yus
gears	gear	gee-yar

handbrake	**brek tangan**	brek ta-ngan
headlights	**lampu depan**	lam-poo dê-pan
ignition	**pencucuhan**	pên-choo-choo-han
ignition key	**kunci pencucuhan**	koon-chee pên-choo-choo-han
indicator	**penunjuk**	pê-noon-juk
lock	**kunci**	koon-chee
radiator	**radiator**	ra-dee-ya-tor
reverse gear	**gear undur**	gee-yar oon-dur
seat belt	**tali pinggang keledar**	ta-lee ping-gang kê-le-dar
spark plug	**palam pencuch**	pa-lam pên-choo-chooh
steering wheel	**roda stereng**	ro-da steh-reng
tyre	**tayar**	ta-yar
wheel	**roda**	ro-da
windscreen	**cermin depan**	chêr-meen dê-pan
windscreen wiper	**pengelap cermin depan**	pê-ngê-lap chêr-meen dê-pan

Road signs

Speed limits are in kilometres per hour. Unless stated otherwise, speed limits are 110 kmph on expressways, 90 kmph on main roads and 60 kmph in urban areas. The majority of Malaysian expressways have tolls.

dilarang membuat pusingan U	dee-la-rang mêm-boo-wat poo-see-ngan yoo	no U-turn
masuk	ma-suk	entrance
keluar	kê-loo-war	exit
lebuh raya	lê-buh ra-ya	motorway
jalan	ja-lan	road
belok kiri	be-lok kee-ree	turn left
belok kanan	be-lok ka-nan	turn right
sehala	sê-ha-la	one way
hujung jalan besar	hoo-jung ja-lan bê-sar	major road ends
dilarang masuk	dee-la-rang ma-suk	no entry
utara	oo-ta-ra	north
selatan	sê-la-tan	south
timur	tee-moor	east
barat	ba-rat	west

lintasan pejalan kaki	leen-ta-san pê-ja-lan ka-kee	pedestrian crossing
pusat bandar	poo-sat ban-dar	city centre
kurangkan laju	koo-rang-kan la-joo	reduce speed
jangan bunyikan hon	ja-ngan boo-nyee-kan hon	no sounding of horn
berhenti	bêr-hên-tee	stop
bahaya	ba-ha-ya	danger
hospital	hos-pee-tal	hospital
dilarang meletak kereta	dee-lah-rang mê-lê-tak kê-re-ta	no parking
ruang letak kereta	roo-wang lê-tak kê-re-ta	parking

Staying somewhere

Hotel (booking)

Malaysia has a wide selection of international, local, luxury and budget hotels and service apartments. Guest houses, inns and youth hostels provide an affordable alternative and can be found in most big towns. Rooms are filled quickly, especially during public and school holidays, so it is advisable to book well in advance. Booking can be done easily via the Internet, telephone or your travel agent.

hotel ho-tel	hotel
rumah tumpangan/ penginapan dan sarapan roo-mah toom-pa-ngan/ pê-ngee-na-pan dan sa-ra-pan	guesthouse/bed and breakfast
bilik kosong/ tiada bilik kosong bee-lik ko-song/tee-ya-da bee-lik ko-song	vacancies/ no vacancies

A **Kami hendak tempah sebuah bilik kelamin**
ka-mee hên-dak têm-pah sê-boo-wah bee-lik
kê-la-min
We would like to book a double room

B **Untuk berapa malam?**
oon-tuk bê-ra-pa ma-lam?
For how many nights?

for 1 night	**untuk satu malam**
	oon-tuk sa-too ma-lam
for 2 nights	**untuk dua malam**
	oon-tuk doo-wa ma-lam
for 1 week	**untuk satu minggu**
	oon-tuk sa-too ming-goo
Is there a hotel/ guesthouse nearby?	**Ada hotel/rumah tumpangan dekat sini?**
	ah-da ho-tel/roo-mah toom-pa-ngan dê-kat see-nee?
Do you have a room?	**Anda ada bilik?**
	an-da ah-da bee-lik?
I'd like...	**Saya mahu...**
	sa-ya ma-hoo...
a single room	**sebuah bilik bujang**
	sê-boo-wah bee-lik boo-jang
a double room	**sebuah bilik kelamin**
	sê-boo-wah bee-lik kê-la-min

Hotel (booking)

53

a room for 3 people	**sebuah bilik untuk tiga orang**
	sê-boo-wah bee-lik oon-tuk tee-ga oh-rang
with shower	**dengan bilik mandi pancuran**
	dê-ngan bee-lik man-dee pan-choo-ran
with bath	**dengan tab mandi**
	dê-ngan tab man-dee
How much is it per night?	**Berapa harganya untuk satu malam?**
	be-ra-pa har-ga-nia oon-tuk sa-too ma-lam?
Is breakfast included?	**Termasuk sarapan pagi?**
	têr-ma-suk sa-ra-pan pa-gee?
I'll be staying...	**Saya akan menginap...**
	sa-ya ah-kan mê-ngee-nap...
We'll be staying...	**Kami akan menginap...**
	ka-mee ah-kan mê-ngee-nap...
1 night	**satu malam**
	sa-too ma-lam
2 nights	**dua malam**
	doo-wa ma-lam
3 nights	**tiga malam**
	tee-ga ma-lam
Is there anywhere else to stay?	**Ada tempat penginapan lain?**
	ah-da têm-pat pê-ngee-na-pan la-yen?

Nama encik, puan? na-ma ên-chik, poo-wan?	Your name, please
Pasport encik, puan? pas-port ên-chik, poo-wan?	Your passport, please
Kami sudah penuh ka-mee soo-dah pê-nuh	We are full

Hotel desk

●●●●●●●●●●●●●●●●●●●●●●●●●●●●●●●●●●●●●

I have a reservation	**Saya ada tempahan** sa-ya ah-da têm-pa-han
My name is...	**Nama saya...** na-ma sa-ya...
Do you have a different room?	**Ada bilik lain?** ah-da bee-lik la-yen?
Where can I park the car?	**Di mana boleh saya letak kereta?** dee ma-na bo-leh sa-ya lê-tak kê-re-ta?
What time is breakfast?	**Sarapan pagi pada pukul berapa?** sa-ra-pan pa-gee pa-da poo-kul bê-ra-pa?

Hotel desk

What time is dinner?	**Makan malam pada pukul berapa?** ma-kan ma-lam pa-da poo-kul bê-ra-pa?
The key, please	**Tolong serahkan kunci** toh-long sê-rah-kan koon-chee
Room number...	**Bilik nombor...** bee-lik nom-bor...
Are there any messages for me?	**Ada apa-apa pesanan untuk saya?** ah-da ah-pa ah-pa pê-sa-nan oon-tuk sa-ya?
I'm leaving tomorrow	**Saya akan berangkat esok** sa-ya ah-kan bêr-ang-kat eh-sok
Please prepare the bill	**Tolong sediakan bil** toh-long sê-di-ya-kan bil
I'd like an early morning call at 7 a.m.	**Saya mahu panggilan bangun tidur pada pukul 7 pagi** sa-ya ma-hoo pang-gee-lan ba-ngoon tee-dur pa-da poo-kul too-juh pa-gee

Camping

tapak perkhemahan ta-pak pêr-khe-ma-han	campsite
air minuman ah-yer mee-noo-man	drinking water
bilik mandi pancuran bee-lik man-dee pan-choo-ran	showers
pejabat pê-ja-bat	office
tempat menyambut tetamu têm-pat mê-nyam-but tê-ta-moo	reception
khemah khe-mah	tent

Where is the camp site?	**Di manakah tapak perkhemahan?** dee ma-na-kah ta-pak pêr-khe-ma-han?
How much is it per night?	**Berapa harganya untuk satu malam?** bê-ra-pa har-ga-nia oon-tuk sa-too ma-lam?
We want to stay...	**Kami hendak menginap...** ka-mee hên-dak mê-ngee-nap...

57

1 night	**satu malam**
	sa-too ma-lam
2 nights	**dua malam**
	doo-wa ma-lam
1 week	**satu minggu**
	sa-too ming-goo
toilets	**tandas**
	tan-das
showers	**bilik mandi pancuran**
	bee-lik man-dee pan-choo-ran
drinking water	**air minuman**
	ah-yer mee-noo-man
Where's the...?	**Di manakah...?**
	dee ma-na-kah...?

YOU MAY HEAR...

| **Kami sudah penuh** | We are full |
| ka-mee soo-dah pê-nuh | |

> **Sightseeing and tourist office** (p 75)

Self-catering

•••••••••••••••••••••••••••••••••

Can you give us an extra set of keys? **Bolehkah anda berikan kami kunci tambahan?**
bo-leh-kah an-da bê-ree-kan ka-mee koon-chi tam-ba-han?

Whom do we contact if there are problems? **Siapakah yang patut dihubungi jika ada masalah?**
see-ya-pa-kah yang pa-tut dee-hoo-boo-ngee jee-ka ah-da ma-sa-lah?

Is there always hot water? **Ada air panas selalu?**
ah-da ah-yer pa-nas sê-la-loo?

Where is the nearest supermarket? **Di manakah pasar raya yang terdekat?**
dee ma-na-kah pa-sar ra-ya yang têr-dê-kat?

Where do we leave the rubbish? **Di mana boleh kami tinggalkan sampah?**
dee ma-na-kah bo-leh ka-mee teeng-gal-kan sam-pah?

> **Sightseeing and tourist office** (p 75)

Self-catering

Shopping

Shopping phrases

• •

Most shops in Malaysia open daily from 9 am to 5 pm.
Malls usually open from 10 am to 10 pm, even on
Sundays. The most popular shopping districts in
Kuala Lumpur are Jalan Bukit Bintang, Jalan Tuanku
Abdul Rahman and Jalan Petaling. You will find
imported, branded products and local goods at the
bigger malls. In some of the smaller shops, it is
possible to negotiate prices with the seller.

FACE TO FACE

A **Saya hendak beli gaun biru**
sa-ya hên-dak bê-lee gown bee-roo
I would like to buy a blue dress

B **Apa saiz anda?**
ah-pa saiz an-da?
What is your size?

A **Saiz lapan belas/dua-puluh**
saiz la-pan bê-las/doo-wa poo-luh
Size 18/20

Where are the shops?	**Di manakah kedai-kedai?**
	dee ma-na-kah kê-dai-kê-dai?
I'm looking for...	**Saya mencari...**
	sa-ya mên-cha-ree...
Where is the nearest...?	**Di manakah ... yang terdekat?**
	dee ma-na-kah ... yang têr-dê-kat?
Where is the nearest baker's?	**Di manakah kedai pembuat roti yang terdekat?**
	dee ma-na-kah kê-dai pêm-boo-wat ro-tee yang têr-dê-kat?
Where is the bazaar?	**Di manakah bazar?**
	dee ma-na-kah ba-zar?
Is it open?	**Ia sudah dibuka?**
	ee-ya soo-dah dee-boo-ka?
When does it close?	**Bilakah ia akan ditutup?**
	bee-la-kah ee-ya ah-kan dee-too-tup?
Can I take that one?	**Boleh saya ambil yang itu?**
	bo-leh sa-ya am-bil yang ee-too?
How much is it?	**Berapa harganya?**
	bê-ra-pa har-ga-nia?
It's too expensive	**Ia terlalu mahal**
	ee-ya têr-lah-loo ma-hal
I don't want it	**Saya tak mahu**
	sa-ya tak ma-hoo

Shops

Where is...?	**Di manakah...?**
	dee ma-na-kah...?
Where is the baker's?	**Di manakah kedai pembuat roti?**
	dee ma-na-kah kê-dai pêm-boo-wat ro-tee?

baker's	**kedai pembuat roti**
	kê-dai pêm-boo-wat ro-tee
bookshop	**kedai buku**
	kê-dai boo-koo
butcher's	**kedai penjual daging**
	kê-dai pên-joo-wal da-ging
cake shop	**kedai kek**
	kê-dai kek
clothes shop	**kedai pakaian**
	kê-dai pa-ka-yan
electrical goods shop	**barangan elektrik**
	ba-ra-ngan ee-lek-trik
fishmonger's	**kedai penjual ikan**
	kê-dai pên-joo-wal ee-kan
furniture shop	**kedai perabot**
	kê-dai pê-ra-bot
gifts/souvenirs	**hadiah/cenderamata**
	ha-dee-yah/cên-dê-ra-ma-ta

greengrocer's	**kedai penjual sayur**
	kê-dai pên-joo-wal sa-yur
grocer's	**kedai runcit**
	kê-dai roon-chit
hairdresser's	**kedai dandan rambut**
	kê-dai dan-dan ram-but
jeweller's	**kedai tukang emas**
	kê-dai too-kang ê-mas
market	**pasar**
	pa-sar
newsagent	**kedai suratkhabar**
	kê-dai soo-rat-kha-bar
optician	**pakar optik**
	pa-kar op-tik
pharmacy	**farmasi**
	far-ma-see
shoe shop	**kedai kasut**
	kê-dai ka-sut
shop	**kedai**
	kê-dai
shopping centre	**pusat membeli-belah**
	poo-sat mêm-bê-lee-bê-lah
spice/herb shop	**kedai rempah/herba**
	kê-dai rêm-pah/hêr-ba
stationer's	**kedai alat tulis**
	kê-dai ah-lat too-lis
supermarket	**pasar raya**
	pa-sar ra-ya

tobacconist's	**kedai penjual barang-barang tembakau**	
	kê-dai pên-joo-wal ba-rang-ba-rang têm-ba-kau	
toy shop	**kedai mainan kanak-kanak**	
	kê-dai mai-nan ka-nak-ka-nak	

Food (general)

bread	roti	ro-tee
butter	mentega	mên-te-ga
cakes	kek	kek
cheese	keju	ke-joo
chicken	ayam	ah-yam
chocolate	cokelat	cho-kê-lat
coffee (instant)	kopi (segera)	ko-pee (sê-gê-ra)
coffee	kopi	ko-pee
crisps	kerepek	kê-re-pek
egg	telur	tê-lur
fish	ikan	ee-kan
flour	tepung	tê-pung
honey	madu	ma-doo
jam	jem	jem
margarine	marjerin	mar-jê-reen
marmalade	marmalad	mar-ma-lad
milk	susu	soo-soo

olive oil	**minyak zaitun**	mee-niak zai-toon
orange juice	**jus oren**	joos oh-ren
pasta	**pasta**	pas-ta
pepper (seasoning)	**lada (perasa)**	la-da (pê-ra-sa)
rice	**nasi**	na-see
salt	**garam**	ga-ram
stock cubes	**kiub perisa**	kee-yoob pê-ree-sa
sugar	**gula**	goo-la
tea	**teh**	teh
vinegar	**cuka**	choo-ka
yoghurt	**yogurt**	yoh-gert

Food (fruit and veg)

Fruit

apples	**epal**	eh-pal
bananas	**pisang**	pee-sang
cherries	**ceri**	che-ree
durian	**durian**	doo-ri-yan
grapes	**anggur**	ang-goor
lime	**limau nipis**	lee-mau nee-pis
longan	**longan**	lo-ngan
mango	**mangga**	mang-ga
mangosteen	**manggis**	mang-gis

melon	**tembikai**	têm-bee-kai
rambutan	**rambutan**	ram-boo-tan
nectarines	**nektarin**	nek-ta-reen
oranges	**oren**	oh-ren
peaches	**pic**	peech
pears	**pear**	per
pineapple	**nenas**	nê-nas
plums	**pelam**	pê-lam
pomegranate	**delima**	dê-lee-ma
strawberries	**stroberi**	stroh-beh-ree
watermelon	**tembikai**	têm-bee-kai

Vegetables

cabbage	**kobis**	ko-bis
carrots	**lobak merah**	lo-bak me-rah
cauliflower	**bunga kobis**	boo-nga ko-bis
cucumber	**timun**	tee-moon
garlic	**bawang putih**	ba-wang poo-tih
green beans	**kacang hijau**	ka-chang hee-jau
lettuce	**daun salad**	da-wun sa-lad
mushrooms	**cendawan**	chen-da-wan
onions	**bawang**	ba-wang
peas	**kacang pis**	ka-chang pis
peppers	**lada benggala**	la-da bêng-ga-la
potatoes	**ubi kentang**	oo-bee kên-tang
spinach	**bayam**	ba-yam
tomatoes	**tomato**	to-ma-to

Clothes

•••

Malaysia uses the same clothing and shoe sizes as the UK. In major clothes stores, you will be able to find clothing and shoes in both UK and US sizes. Malaysian clothing and shoe sizes:

Women's sizes

UK	Malaysia
10	10 **sepuluh** (sê-poo-luh)
12	12 **dua belas** (doo-wa bê-las)
14	14 **empat belas** (êm-pat bê-las)
16	16 **enam belas** (ê-nam bê-las)
18	18 **lapan belas** (la-pan bê-las)
20	20 **dua-puluh** (doo-wa poo-luh)

Men's suit sizes

UK	Malaysia
36	36 **tiga-puluh enam** (tee-ga poo-luh ê-nam)
38	38 **tiga-puluh lapan** (tee-ga poo-luh la-pan)
40	40 **empat-puluh** (êm-pat poo-luh)
42	42 **empat-puluh dua** (êm-pat poo-luh doo-wa)
44	44 **empat-puluh empat** (êm-pat poo-luh êm-pat)
46	46 **empat-puluh enam** (êm-pat poo-luh ê-nam)

Shoe sizes

UK	Malaysia		
2	2	**dua**	(doo-wa)
3	3	**tiga**	(tee-ga)
4	4	**empat**	(êm-pat)
5	5	**lima**	(lee-ma)
6	6	**enam**	(ê-nam)
7	7	**tujuh**	(too-juh)
8	8	**lapan**	(la-pan)
9	9	**sembilan**	(sêm-bee-lan)
10	10	**sepuluh**	(sê-poo-luh)
11	11	**sebelas**	(sê-bê-las)

FACE TO FACE

A Boleh saya cuba yang ini?

bo-leh sa-ya choo-ba yang ee-nee?

Can I try this one on?

B Ya, sudah tentu, anda boleh cuba di sini

ya, soo-dah tên-too, an-da bo-leh choo-ba dee see-nee

Yes, of course, you can try it on in here

Is there a small/ medium/large size for this one?	**Ada saiz kecil/sederhana/ besar untuk ini?** ah-da saiz kê-chil/sê-dêr-ha-na/ bê-sar oon-tuk ee-nee?

68

Yes, there is	**Ya, ada**
	ya, ah-da
No, there isn't	**Tak ada**
	tak ah-da
Is it real leather?	**Ini kulit betul?**
	ee-nee koo-lit bê-tool?
Do you have this one in other colours?	**Ada warna lain?**
	ah-da war-na la-yen?
It's too expensive	**Ia terlalu mahal**
	ee-ya têr-la-loo ma-hal
It's too big	**Ia terlalu besar**
	ee-ya têr-la-loo bê-sar
It's too small	**Ia terlalu kecil**
	ee-ya têr-la-loo kê-chil
No thanks, I don't want it	**Terima kasih, saya tak mahu**
	tê-ree-ma ka-sih, sa-ya tak ma-hoo

Clothes (articles)

● ●

cotton	**kapas**	ka-pas
leather	**kulit**	koo-lit
silk	**sutera**	soo-tê-ra
wool	**bulu**	boo-loo
coat	**kot**	kowt

dress	**gaun**	gown
hat	**topi**	to-pee
jacket	**jaket**	ja-ket
knickers	**seluar dalam**	sê-loo-war da-lam
	wanita	wa-nee-ta
sandals	**sandal**	san-dal
shirt	**kemeja**	kê-me-ja
shorts	**seluar pendek**	sê-loo-war pen-dek
skirt	**skirt**	skirt
socks	**stokin**	sto-kin
swimsuit	**baju renang**	ba-joo rê-nang
T-shirt	**baju t**	ba-joo tee
trousers	**seluar**	sê-loo-war
underpants	**seluar dalam**	sê-loo-war da-lam

Maps and guides

Free maps of Malaysia and specific destinations are available at any Tourism Malaysia office around the world and in Malaysia. In Kuala Lumpur, the office is located at the Putra World Trade Centre at Jalan Tun Ismail. You will be given a welcome package that contains detailed maps and directions to major attractions. You can also find maps at the bigger hotels, airports and bus and train stations.

> **Paying** (p 97)

Where can I buy a map?	**Di manakah boleh saya beli peta?**
	dee ma-na-kah bo-leh sa-ya bê-lee pê-ta?
Do you have a road map?	**Anda ada peta jalan?**
	an-da ah-da pê-ta ja-lan?
Do you have a town plan?	**Anda ada pelan bandar?**
	an-da ah-da pê-lan ban-dar?
Do you have a leaflet/ guidebook in English?	**Anda ada risalah/buku panduan dalam Bahasa Inggeris?**
	an-da ah-da ree-sa-lah/boo-koo pan-doo-wan da-lam ba-ha-sa ing-gê-ris?
Can you show me where ... is on the map?	**Anda boleh tunjuk di mana ... pada peta?**
	an-da bo-leh toon-juk dee ma-na ... pa-da pê-ta?
Where can I buy a newspaper?	**Di manakah boleh saya beli suratkhabar?**
	dee ma-na-kah bo-leh sa-ya bê-lee soo-rat-kha-bar?
Have you any English newspapers?	**Anda ada suratkabar Bahasa Inggeris?**
	an-da ah-da soo-rat-kha-bar ba-ha-sa ing-gê-ris?

Maps and guides

> **Asking the way** (p 25)

Post office

Post offices are open from 8.30 am to 5 pm from Monday to Friday. Besides the ordinary mailing services, Pos Malaysia also provides a domestic and international courier service, called Poslaju or Expedited Mail Service (EMS). The offices of private international couriers like DHL and UPS can also be found in major urban locations.

mel udara mel oo-da-ra	airmail
luar negara loo-war ne-ga-ra	overseas
pedalaman pê-da-la-man	inland
tempatan têm-pa-tan	local
surat soo-rat	letter
poskad pos-kad	postcard
setem sê-tem	stamps

Where is the post office?	**Di manakah pejabat pos?** dee ma-na-kah pê-ja-bat pos?
Where can I buy stamps?	**Di manakah boleh saya beli setem?** dee ma-na-kah bo-leh sa-ya bê-lee sê-tem?

5 stamps	**lima keping setem**
	lee-ma kêping sê-tem
10 stamps	**sepuluh keping setem**
	sê-poo-luh kê-ping sê-tem
for postcards	**untuk poskad**
	oon-tuk pos-kad
for letters	**untuk surat**
	oon-tuk soo-rat
to Britain	**ke Britain**
	kê bri-tên
to America	**ke Amerika**
	kê ah-me-ree-ka
to Australia	**ke Australia**
	kê os-tra-li-ya

Photos

Where is there a photographic shop?	**Di manakah kedai foto?**
	dee ma-na-kah kê-dai fo-to?
I need a film for this camera	**Saya perlu filem untuk kamera ini**
	sa-ya pêr-loo fee-lêm oon-tuk ka-me-ra ee-nee

> **Money** (p 96) > **Paying** (p 97)

73

I need batteries for this	**Saya perlu bateri untuk ini** sa-ya pêr-loo ba-tê-ree oon-tuk ee-nee
I'd like these films developed	**Saya hendak cuci filem ini** sa-ya hên-dak choo-chee fee-lêm ee-nee
How long will it take?	**Berapa lama?** bê-ra-pa la-ma?
How much will it cost?	**Berapa harganya?** bê-ra-pa har-ga-nia?

Leisure

Sightseeing and tourist office

Tourists can drop in at any Tourism Malaysia office, where they will find welcome packages filled with useful information.

maklumat mak-loo-mat	information
pejabat pelancong pê-ja-bat pê-lan-chong	tourist office
muzium moo-zee-yoom	museum
galeri lukisan ga-lê-ree loo-ki-san	art gallery
kuil koo-wil	temple
lawatan berpandu la-wa-tan bêr-pan-doo	guided tour
tiket tee-ket	tickets
tandas tan-das	toilet

Where is the tourist office?	**Di manakah pejabat pelancong?**
	dee ma-na-kah pê-ja-bat pê-lan-chong?
What can we visit in the area?	**Bila boleh kami lawat kawasan itu?**
	bee-la bo-leh ka-mee la-wat ka-wa-san ee-too?
Have you got details in English?	**Anda ada butir-butir dalam bahasa Inggeris?**
	an-da ah-da boo-tir-boo-tir da-lam ba-ha-sa ing-gê-ris?
Are there any excursions?	**Ada tak lawatan ke mana-mana?**
	ah-da tak la-wa-tan kê ma-na-ma-na?
When does it leave?	**Bilakah ia akan berlepas?**
	bee-la-kah ee-ya ah-kan bêr-lê-pas?
When does it get back?	**Bilakah ia akan kembali?**
	bee-la-kah ee-ya ah-kan kêm-ba-lee?

> **Maps and guides** (p 70)

Entertainment

•••••••••••••••••••••••••••••••••••

What is there to do in the evenings?	**Petang-petang boleh buat apa?** pê-tang pê-tang bo-leh boo-wat ah-pa?
We would like to go to a disco	**Kami ingin pergi ke disko** ka-mee ee-ngin pêr-gee kê dis-ko
Is there anywhere we can go to hear live music?	**Ada tak tempat untuk menikmati muzik secara 'live'?** ah-da tak têm-pat oon-tuk mê-nik-ma-tee moo-zik sê-cha-ra laiv?
Is there anywhere we can go to see Malay dancing?	**Ada tak tempat untuk menonton tarian Melayu?** ah-da tak têm-pat oon-tuk mê-non-ton ta-ree-yan mê-la-yoo?
Is there any entertainment for children?	**Ada tak hiburan untuk kanak-kanak?** ah-da tak hee-boo-ran oon-tuk ka-nak-ka-nak?

Leisure/beach

pantai	pan-tai	beach
bahaya	ba-ha-ya	danger
bilik mandi pancuran		showers
bee-lik man-dee		
pan-choo-ran		

Are there any good beaches round here?	**Ada tak pantai yang cantik-cantik di sini?**
	ah-da tak pan-tai yang chan-tik-chan-tik dee see-nee?
Is there a bus (taxi) to the beach?	**Ada tak bas (teksi) yang menuju ke pantai?**
	ah-da tak bas (tek-see) yang mê-noo-joo kê pan-tai?
Can we go windsurfing?	**Boleh tak kami pergi meluncur angin?**
	bo-leh tak ka-mee pêr-gee mê-loon-choor ah-ngin?
Please go away!	**Tolong pergi dari sini!**
	to-long pêr-gee da-ree see-nee!

> **Sport** (p 84) > **Walking** (p 85)

Leisure

Music

....

Is there anywhere we can go to hear music?	**Ada tak tempat di mana kami boleh mendengar muzik?**
	ah-da tak têm-pat dee ma-na ka-mee bo-leh mên-dê-ngar moo-zik?
Are there any concerts?	**Ada tak apa-apa konsert?**
	ah-da tak ah-pa-ah-pa kon-sêrt?
Where can I get tickets?	**Di mana boleh saya dapatkan tiket?**
	dee ma-na bo-leh sa-ya da-pat-kan tee-ket?
Where can I hear some classical music/jazz?	**Di mana boleh saya dengar muzik klasik/jazz?**
	dee ma-na bo-leh sa-ya dê-ngar moo-zik kla-sik/jazz?

Cinema

....

| **panggung wayang** pang-goong wa-yang | cinema |
| **tayangan** ta-ya-ngan | screening |

> **Making friends** (p 20)

What's on at the cinema?	**Apa yang sedang ditayangkan di panggung?**
	ah-pa yang sê-dang dee-ta-yang-kan dee pang-goong?
What time does the film start?	**Pada pukul berapa wayang akan bermula?**
	pa-da poo-kul bê-ra-pa wa-yang ah-kan bêr-moo-la?
How much are the tickets?	**Berapakah harga tiket?**
	bê-ra-pa-kah har-ga tee-ket?
Two for ... (name and time of performance) showing	**Dua tiket untuk tayangan...**
	doo-wa tee-ket oon-tuk ta-ya-ngan...

YOU MAY HEAR...

Kami sudah kehabisan tiket untuk tayangan... ka-mee soo-dah kê-ha-bee-san tee-ket oon-tuk ta-ya-ngan...	For screening ... we have no tickets left

Mosque

•••

Women and girls should have their heads and
shoulders covered, and both male and female
visitors should avoid wearing shorts. You will have
to leave your shoes at the entrance. Refrain from
eating or drinking inside the mosque. Prayers take
place five times a day and it would be best to wait
until these are over before entering.

masjid mas-jid	mosque
muslim moos-lim	Muslim
kristian kris-tee-yan	Christian
kasut ka-sut	shoes
dilarang menangkap foto dee-la-rang mê-nang-kap foto	no photos
dilarang membuat rakaman video dee-la-rang mêm-boo-wat ra-ka-man vee-dee-yo	no videos

I'd like to see the mosque	**Saya mahu tengok masjid** sa-ya ma-hoo te-ngok mas-jid

When can we see the mosque?	**Bila boleh kami tengok masjid?**
	bee-la bo-leh ka-mee te-ngok mas-jid?
Where is the mosque?	**Dimanakah masjid?**
	dee-ma-na-kah mas-jid?

Television

Besides RTM 1 and RTM 2, which are the government-owned TV channels, there are also several free-to-air private stations and a pay-to-view network called ASTRO. The stations broadcast a variety of shows in many languages, including English, and you can enjoy both local productions and programmes from other countries.

kawalan jauh ka-wa-lan ja-wuh	remote control
berita bê-ree-ta	news
untuk menghidupkan oon-tuk mêng-hee-dup-kan	to switch on
untuk mematikan oon-tuk mê-ma-tee-kan	to switch off
kartun ka-toon	cartoons

Where is the television?	**Di manakah televisyen?**
	dee ma-na-kah te-le-vee-shên?
How do I switch on the television?	**Bagaimana cara untuk menghidupkan televisyen?**
	ba-gai-ma-na cha-ra oon-tuk mêng-hee-dup-kan te-le-vee-shên?
What's on television?	**Apa yang sedang disiarkan di televisyen?**
	ah-pa yang sê-dang dee-see-yar-kan dee te-le-vee-shên?
Are there any English-speaking channels?	**Ada tak saluran bahasa Inggeris?**
	ah-da tak sa-loo-ran ba-ha-sa ing-ge-ris?
Are there any children's programmes?	**Ada rancangan untuk kanak-kanak?**
	ah-da tak ran-cha-ngan oon-tuk ka-nak-ka-nak?
When is the football on?	**Bilakah waktu siaran perlawanan bola sepak?**
	bee-la-kah wak-too see-ya-ran pêr-la-wa-nan bo-la se-pak?
When is the news on?	**Bilakah waktu siaran berita?**
	bee-la-kah wak-too see-ya-ran bê-ree-ta?

Sport

Where can we play tennis?	**Di mana boleh kami main tenis?** dee ma-na bo-leh ka-mee ma-yin te-nis?
Where can we play golf?	**Di mana boleh kami main golf?** dee ma-na bo-leh ka-mee ma-yin golf?
Where can we play football?	**Di mana boleh kami main bola sepak?** dee ma-na bo-leh ka-mee ma-yin bo-la se-pak?
Can we play tennis/golf?	**Boleh kami main tenis/golf?** bo-leh ka-mee ma-yin te-nis/golf?
Can we hire rackets/golf clubs?	**Boleh kami sewa raket/kayu golf?** bo-leh ka-mee seh-wa ra-ket/ka-yoo golf?
How much is it per hour?	**Berapa harganya untuk sejam?** bê-ra-pa har-ga-nia oon-tuk sê-jam?

Can we watch a football match?	**Boleh kami tonton perlawanan bola sepak?**
	bo-leh ka-mee ton-ton pêr-la-wa-nan bo-la se-pak?
Where can we get tickets?	**Di manakah boleh kami dapatkan tiket?**
	dee ma-na-kah bo-leh ka-mee da-pat-kan tee-ket?
How do we get to the stadium?	**Bagaimana cara untuk pergi ke stadium?**
	ba-gai-ma-na cha-ra oon-tuk pêr-gee kê sta-dee-yoom?

Walking

Are there any guided walks?	**Ada tak aktiviti bersiar-siar berpandu?**
	ah-da tak ak-tee-vee-tee bêr-see-yar-see-yar bêr-pan-doo?
Do you have a guide to local walks?	**Anda ada pemandu untuk bersiar-siar di kawasan setempat?**
	an-da ah-da pê-man-doo oon-tuk bêr-see-yar-see-yar dee ka-wa-san sê-têm-pat?

How many kilometres is the walk?	**Berapa kilometer perjalanannya?**
	be-ra-pa kee-lo-mee-têr pêr-ja-la-nan-nia?
How long will it take?	**Berapa lama?**
	bê-ra-pa la-ma?
Is it very steep?	**Curam tak?**
	choo-ram tak?
I'd like to go climbing	**Saya ingin mendaki**
	sa-ya ee-ngin mên-da-kee

Leisure

Communications

Telephone and mobile

A variety of phonecards can be bought at any Telekom Malaysia outlet. They are also widely available in shopping malls, and even smaller sundry shops. If you are planning to call overseas, be sure to buy a phonecard that will allow you to do so. The phonecard will usually come with instructions on how to place a call. To call Malaysia from abroad, dial oo followed by 6o then the area code and phone number. A call to Kuala Lumpur, for example, would be oo-6o-3-phone number.

kad panggilan kad pang-gee-lan	phonecard
buku telefon boo-koo te-le-fon	telephone directory
panggilan pindah **bayaran** pang-gee-lan peen-dah ba-ya-ran	reverse charges (collect)
kod pendailan kod pên-dai-lan	dialling code

Hello, I am...	**Helo, saya...**
	he-lo, sa-ya...
I would like to speak to...	**Saya mahu bercakap dengan...**
	sa-ya ma-hoo bêr-cha-kap dê-ngan...
I want to make a phone call	**Saya hendak membuat panggilan telefon**
	sa-ya hên-dak mêm-boo-wat pang-gee-lan te-le-fon
I want to phone (country name)	**Saya hendak menelefon** (country name)
	sa-ya hên-dak mê-ne-le-fon (country name)
An outside line, please	**Tolong hubungkan saya dengan talian luar**
	toh-long hoo-bung-kan sa-ya dê-ngan ta-lee-yan loo-war
Where can I buy a phonecard?	**Di mana boleh saya beli kad panggilan?**
	dee ma-na bo-leh sa-ya bê-lee kad pang-gee-lan?
Please write the phone number down	**Sila catatkan nombor telefon itu**
	see-la cha-tat-kan nom-bor te-le-fon ee-too
Do you have a mobile phone?	**Anda ada telefon bimbit?**
	an-da ah-da te-le-fon beem-bit?

Can I speak to...?	**Boleh saya bercakap dengan...?**
	bo-leh sa-ya bêr-cha-kap dê-ngan...?
This is...	**Ini...**
	ee-nee...
I'll call back later	**Saya akan telefon lagi nanti**
	sa-ya ah-kan te-le-fon la-gee nan-tee
I'll call again tomorrow	**Saya akan telefon lagi esok**
	sa-ya ah-kan te-le-fon la-gee eh-sok

YOU MAY HEAR...

Helo he-lo	Hello
Tunggu sebentar toong-goo sê-bên-tar	Please hold on
Siapa di sana? see-ya-pa dee sa-na?	Who is calling?
Boleh telefon lagi nanti? bo-leh te-le-fon la-gee nan-tee?	Can you call back later?
Anda hendak tinggalkan pesanan? an-da hên-dak teeng-gal-kan pê-sa-nan?	Do you want to leave a message?
Salah nombor sa-lah nom-bor	Wrong number

Telephone and mobile

89

Text messaging

I will text you	**Saya akan hantar SMS kepada anda**
	sa-ya ah-kan han-tar es-em-es kê-pa-da an-da
Can you text me?	**Boleh anda hantar SMS kepada saya?**
	bo-leh an-da han-tar es-em-es kê-pa-da sa-ya?
Did you get my text message?	**Anda dapat pesanan teks saya?**
	an-da da-pat pê-sa-nan tex sa-ya?
Can you send me a picture with your mobile?	**Bolehkah anda hantar gambar kepada saya dengan telefon bimbit anda?**
	bo-leh-kah an-da han-tar gam-bar kê-pa-da sa-ya dê-ngan te-le-fon beem-bit an-da?
Hello? (to answer the phone)	**Helo?**
	he-lo?
See you	**Jumpa nanti**
	joom-pa nan-tee
tomorrow	**esok**
	eh-sok
Please call me	**sila hubungi saya**
	see-la hoo-boo-ngee sa-ya

Communications

today	**hari ini**
	ha-ree ee-nee
too late	**terlalu lambat**
	têr-la-loo lam-bat
tonight	**malam ini**
	ma-lam ee-nee
Text me	**hantar pesanan teks kepada saya**
	han-tar pê-sa-nan tex kê-pa-da sa-ya
Free to talk?	**Boleh berbual?**
	bo-leh bêr-boo-wal?
I'll call you back later	**Saya akan telefon anda nanti**
	sa-ya ah-kan te-le-fon an-da nan-tee
Thanks	**Terima kasih**
	tê-ree-ma ka-sih
Are you OK?	**Anda sihat?**
	an-da see-hat?

E-mail

The TLD (internet suffix) for Malaysia is '.com.my'

Do you have e-mail?	**Anda ada alamat e-mel?** an-da ah-da ah-la-mat ee-mel?
My e-mail address is...	**Alamat e-mel saya ialah...** ah-la-mat ee-mel sa-ya ee-ya-lah...
What is your e-mail address?	**Apakah alamat e-mel anda?** ah-pa-kah ah-la-mat ee-mel an-da?
How do you spell it?	**Bagaimana hendak mengejanya?** ba-gai-ma-na hên-dak mê-nge-ja-nia?
All one word	**Semua satu perkataan** sê-moo-wa sa-too pêr-ka-ta-an
All lower case	**Semua huruf kecil** sê-moo-wa hoo-ruf kê-chil
Can I send an e-mail?	**Boleh saya hantar e-mel?** bo-leh sa-ya han-tar ee-mel?
Did you get my e-mail?	**Anda terima e-mel saya?** an-da tê-ree-ma ee-mel sa-ya?

Internet

•••••••••••••••••••••••••••••••••••••••

Cyber cafés are easy to locate in the bigger cities.
Larger hotels usually provide Internet access in
their business centres and, if you bring your own
laptop, you can request Internet access in the
privacy of your own room.

rerumah rê-roo-mah	home
nama pengguna na-ma pêng-goo-na	username
untuk menyemak imbas oon-tuk mê-nyeh-mak eem-bas	to browse
enjin carian en-jeen cha-ree-yan	search engine
kata laluan ka-ta la-loo-wan	password
hubungi kami hoo-boo-ngee ka-mee	contact us
kembali ke menu kêm-ba-lee kê me-noo	back to menu
peta tapak pê-ta ta-pak	sitemap

Internet

Are there any Internet cafés here?	**Ada tak kafe Internet di sini?** ah-da tak ka-fey in-têr-net dee see-nee?
How much is it to log on for an hour?	**Berapa harganya untuk log masuk selama sejam?** bê-ra-pa har-ga-nia oon-tuk log ma-suk sê-la-ma sê-jam?
I would like to print some pages	**Saya mahu cetak beberapa muka surat** sa-ya ma-hoo chê-tak bê-bê-ra-pa moo-ka soo-rat

Fax

. . . .

Most hotels have business centres that offer fax services.

daripada da-ree-pa-da	from
kepada kê-pa-da	to
tarikh ta-rikh	date
... muka surat termasuk yang ini... ... moo-ka soo-rat têr-ma-sook yang ee-nee...	... pages including this

I want to send a fax	**Saya hendak hantar faks**
	sa-ya hên-dak han-tar fax
Do you have a fax?	**Anda ada faks?**
	an-da ah-da fax?
Where can I send a fax?	**Di mana boleh saya hantar faks?**
	dee ma-na bo-leh sa-ya han-tar fax?
How much is it to send a fax?	**Berapa harganya untuk menghantar faks?**
	bê-ra-pa har-ga-nia oon-tuk mêng-han-tar fax?
What is your fax number?	**Apakah nombor faks anda?**
	ah-pa-kah nom-bor fax an-da?
The fax number is...	**Nombor faksnya ialah...**
	nom-bor fax-nia ee-ya-lah...

Practicalities

Money

The Malaysian currency is the Ringgit (RM). Banks are open from 9.15 am to 4 pm on weekdays. In Kedah, Kelantan and Terengganu, banks are closed on Fridays. You can change money at the airport, banks and hotels, but look out for authorized money-changers in shopping malls and smaller stores. They often offer better rates.

Where is the nearest bank?	**Di manakah bank yang terdekat?**
	dee ma-na-kah benk yang têr-dê-kat?
Where is the nearest currency office?	**Di manakah kaunter pertukaran wang yang terdekat?**
	dee ma-na-kah kaun-têr pêr-too-ka-ran wang yang têr-dê-kat?

Can I change money here?	**Boleh saya tukar wang di sini?**
	bo-leh sa-ya too-kar wang dee see-nee?
What is the exchange rate?	**Apakah kadar pertukaran?**
	ah-pa-kah ka-dar pêr-too-ka-ran?
I want to change £50	**Saya hendak tukar lima-puluh paun**
	sa-ya hên-dak too-kar lee-ma poo-luh pa-wun
I want to buy Travellers Cheques	**Saya hendak beli cek kembara**
	sa-ya hên-dak bê-lee chek kêm-ba-ra

Paying

•••

Major credit cards are accepted at most larger stores, hotels and restaurants. Beware of credit card fraud and cloning and keep a close watch on your credit card during transactions.

bil	bil	bill
resit	reh-sit	receipt
invois	in-vois	invoice
meja tunai	me-ja too-nai	cash desk
kad kredit	kad kreh-dit	credit card

I'd like to pay now	**Saya mahu bayar sekarang**
	sa-ya ma-hoo ba-yar sê-ka-rang
How much is it?	**Berapa harganya?**
	bê-ra-pa har-ga-nia?
Can I pay...?	**Boleh saya bayar...?**
	bo-leh sa-ya ba-yar...?
Can I pay by credit card/ cheque?	**Boleh saya bayar dengan kad kredit/cek?**
	bo-leh sa-ya ba-yar dê-ngan kad kreh-deet/chek?
by credit card	**dengan kad kredit**
	dê-ngan kad kreh-deet
with Travellers Cheques	**dengan cek kembara**
	dê-ngan chek kêm-ba-ra
Where do I pay?	**Bayar di mana?**
	ba-yar dee ma-na?
Please write down the price	**Sila catatkan harganya**
	see-la cha-tat-kan har-ga-nia
Put it on my bill (in a hotel)	**Masukkan dalam bil saya**
	ma-suk-kan da-lam bil sa-ya
I'd like a receipt, please	**Tolong beri saya resit**
	toh-long bê-ree sa-ya reh-sit
I think there is a mistake	**Saya rasa ada kesilapan**
	sa-ya ra-sa ah-da kê-see-la-pan
Keep the change	**Simpan bakinya**
	seem-pan ba-kee-nia

> **Shopping** (p 60)

Luggage

beg pakaian beg pa-ka-yan	suitcase
beg tangan beg ta-ngan	handbag
beg bimbit beg beem-bit	briefcase
bagasi tangan ba-ga-see ta-ngan	hand luggage
pejabat simpan bagasi pê-ja-bat sim-pan ba-ga-see	left-luggage office
loker lo-ker	locker
troli tro-lee	trolley

My suitcase hasn't arrived	**Beg pakaian saya belum tiba** beg pa-ka-yan sa-ya bê-lum tee-ba
My suitcase is missing	**Beg pakaian saya hilang** beg pa-ka-yan sa-ya hee-lang
My suitcase is damaged	**Beg pakaian saya rosak** beg pa-ka-yan sa-ya ro-sak
Can I leave my suitcase here?	**Boleh saya tinggalkan beg pakaian saya di sini?** bo-leh sa-ya teeng-gal-kan beg pa-ka-yan sa-ya dee see-ni?
Is there a left-luggage office?	**Ada tak pejabat simpan bagasi?** ah-da tak pê-ja-bat sim-pan ba-ga-see?

Luggage

When does it open?	**Bilakah ia dibuka?**
	bee-la-kah ee-ya ah-kan dee-boo-ka?
When does it close?	**Bilakah ia akan ditutup?**
	bee-la-kah ee-ya ah-kan dee-too-tup?

Repairs

kedai baiki kasut	shoe repair shop
kê-dai bai-kee ka-soot	
baiki sementara anda tunggu	repairs while you wait
bai-kee sê-mên-ta-ra an-da toong-goo	

This is broken	**Ini rosak**
	ee-nee ro-sak
Where can I get this repaired?	**Ke mana boleh saya hantarkan untuk dibaiki?**
	kê ma-na bo-leh sa-ya han-tar-kan oon-tuk dee-bai-kee?
Can you repair...?	**Boleh anda baiki...?**
	bo-leh an-da bai-kee...?

> **Train** (p 32) > **Air travel** (p 39)

my glasses?	**cermin mata saya?**
	chêr-min ma-ta sa-ya?
my camera?	**kamera saya?**
	ka-me-ra sa-ya?
How much will it cost?	**Berapa harganya?**
	bê-ra-pa har-ga-nia?
How long will it take?	**Berapa lama?**
	be-ra-pa la-ma?

YOU MAY HEAR...

| **Saya tak boleh membaikinya**
sa-ya tak bo-leh mêm-bai-kee-nia | I cannot repair this |

Laundry

serbuk pencuci sêr-buk pên-choo-chee	washing powder
kedai dobi layan-diri kê-dai doh-bee la-yan dee-ree	launderette
kedai dobi cuci kering kê-dai doh-bee choo-chee kê-ring	dry cleaner's

> **Breakdown** (p 47)

Where can I wash some clothes?	**Di mana boleh saya cuci pakaian?**
	dee ma-na bo-leh sa-ya choo-chee pa-ka-yan?
Do you have a laundry service?	**Anda ada khidmat dobi?**
	an-da ah-da khid-mat doh-bee?
Where is the launderette?	**Di manakah kedai dobi layan-diri?**
	dee ma-na-kah kê-dai doh-bee la-yan dee-ree?
Where is the dry cleaner's?	**Di manakah kedai dobi cuci kering?**
	dee ma-na-kah kê-dai doh-bee choo-chee kê-ring?
Can I borrow an iron?	**Boleh saya pinjam seterika?**
	bo-leh sa-ya peen-jam sê-tê-ree-ka?

YOU MAY HEAR...

untuk setiap item	per item
oon-tuk sê-tee-yap ai-têm	

Complaints

●●●●●●●●●●●●●●●●●●●●●●●●●●●●●●●●●●●●●●

This doesn't work	**Ini tidak berfungsi**
	ee-nee tee-dak bêr-foong-see
The room is dirty	**Bilik ini kotor**
	bee-lik ee-nee ko-tor
The room is too hot	**Bilik ini panas**
	bee-lik ee-nee pa-nas
I didn't order this	**Saya tidak memesannya**
	sa-ya tee-dak mê-mê-san-nia
I want to complain	**Saya hendak buat aduan**
	sa-ya hên-dak boo-wat ah-doo-wan
Please call the manager	**Tolong panggil pengurus**
	toh-long pang-gil pê-ngoo-roos
... out of order	**... rosak**
	... ro-sak
toilet	**tandas**
	tan-das
shower	**bilik mandi pancuran**
	bee-lik man-dee pan-choo-ran
television	**televisyen**
	te-le-vee-shên

> **Hotel desk** (p 55)

Complaints

Problems

●●

Can you help me?	**Boleh anda bantu saya?**
	bo-leh an-da ban-too sa-ya?
I don't speak Malay	**Saya tidak boleh bertutur dalam Bahasa Melayu**
	sa-ya tee-dak bo-leh bêr-too-tur da-lam ba-ha-sa mê-la-yoo
Do you speak English?	**Anda boleh bertutur dalam bahasa Inggeris?**
	an-da bo-leh bêr-too-tur da-lam ba-ha-sa ing-gê-ris?
Is there someone who speaks English?	**Ada tak orang yang boleh bertutur dalam bahasa Inggeris?**
	ah-da tak o-rang yang bo-leh bêr-too-tur da-lam ba-ha-sa ing-gê-ris?
I'm lost	**Saya sesat jalan**
	sa-ya sê-sat ja-lan
I need to go to...	**Saya ingin pergi ke...**
	sa-ya ee-ngin pêr-gee kê...
the station	**stesen**
	steh-sen
my hotel	**hotel saya**
	ho-tel sa-ya

this address	**alamat ini**
	a-la-mat ee-nee
I've missed my train	**Saya ketinggalan keretapi**
	sa-ya kê-teeng-ga-lan kê-re-ta-pee
I've missed my bus	**Saya ketinggalan bas**
	sa-ya kê-teeng-ga-lan bas
I've missed my plane	**Saya ketinggalan kapalterbang**
	sa-ya kê-teeng-ga-lan ka-pal-têr-bang
I've missed the connecting bus	**Saya ketinggalan bas penyambung**
	sa-ya kê-teeng-ga-lan bas pê-nyam-bung
I've missed the connecting train	**Saya ketinggalan keretapi penyambung**
	sa-ya kê-teeng-ga-lan kê-re-ta-pee pê-nyam-bung
I've missed the connecting plane	**Saya ketinggalan kapalterbang penyambung**
	sa-ya kê-teeng-ga-lan ka-pal-têr-bang pê-nyam-bung
The coach has left without me	**Saya ketinggalan bas**
	sa-ya kê-teeng-ga-lan bas
How does this work?	**Bagaimana ini berfungsi?**
	ba-gai-ma-na ee-nee bêr-foong-see?

| That man is following me | **Lelaki itu mengekori saya** lê-la-kee ee-too mê-nge-ko-ree sa-ya |
| I lost my money | **Saya kehilangan duit** sa-ya kê-hee-la-ngan doo-wit |

Emergencies

polis po-lis	police
bomba bom-ba	fire brigade
ambulan am-boo-lan	ambulance
hospital hos-pee-tal	hospital
Tolong! toh-long!	Help!
Api! ah-pee!	Fire!

There's been an accident	**Ada kemalangan** ah-da kê-ma-la-ngan
Please help me	**Tolong saya** toh-long sa-ya
Please call the police/fire brigade	**Tolong panggil polis/bomba** toh-long pang-gil po-lis/bom-ba
Someone has been injured	**Ada orang tercedera** ah-da o-rang têr-chê-dê-ra

Where is the police station?	**Di manakah stesen polis yang terdekat?**
	dee ma-na-kah steh-sen po-lis yang têr-dê-kat?
I've been robbed	**Saya telah dirompak**
	sa-ya tê-lah dee-rom-pak
I've been raped	**Saya telah dirogol**
	sa-ya tê-lah dee-ro-gol
I want to speak to a policewoman	**Saya hendak bercakap dengan polis wanita**
	sa-ya hên-dak bêr-cha-kap dê-ngan po-lis wa-nee-ta
Someone has stolen...	**Ada orang curi...**
	ah-da oh-rang choo-ree...
I've lost...	**Saya kehilangan...**
	sa-ya kê-hee-la-ngan...
my money	**duit saya**
	doo-wit sa-ya
my passport	**pasport saya**
	pas-port sa-ya
my plane ticket	**tiket penerbangan saya**
	tee-ket pê-nêr-ba-ngan sa-ya
My son is missing	**Anak lelaki saya hilang**
	ah-nak lê-la-kee sa-ya hee-lang
My daughter is missing	**Anak perempuan saya hilang**
	ah-nak pê-rêm-poo-wan sa-ya hee-lang

Emergencies

His/Her name is...	**Namanya...**
	na-ma-nia...
I need a report for my insurance	**Saya perlukan laporan untuk insuran saya**
	sa-ya pêr-loo-kan la-po-ran oon-tuk in-soo-ran sa-ya
Please call the British Embassy	**Tolong telefon Kedutaan British**
	toh-long te-le-fon kê-doo-ta-an bri-tish
Please call the Australian Embassy	**Tolong telefon Kedutaan Australia**
	toh-long te-le-fon kê-doo-ta-an os-tra-li-ya
Please call the Canadian Embassy	**Tolong telefon Kedutaan Kanada**
	toh-long te-le-fon kê-doo-ta-an ka-na-da

Health

Pharmacy

Pharmacies can be found throughout Malaysia. The larger ones are usually open from 9 am to 7 pm or later.

Where is the nearest pharmacy?	**Di manakah farmasi yang terdekat?**
	dee ma-na-kah far-ma-see yang têr-dê-kat?
I need something...	**Saya perlukan sesuatu...**
	sa-ya pêr-loo-kan sê-soo-wa-too...
for diarrhoea	**untuk cirit-birit**
	oon-tuk che-ret-be-ret
for constipation	**untuk sembelit**
	oon-tuk sêm-bê-lit
for food poisoning	**untuk keracunan makanan**
	oon-tuk kê-ra-choo-nan ma-ka-nan
Is it safe for...?	**Selamat untuk...?**
	sê-la-mat oon-tuk...?

children	**kanak-kanak**
	ka-nak ka-nak
I am pregnant	**Saya hamil**
	sa-ya ha-mil
What is the dose?	**Berapa banyak dosnya?**
	bê-ra-pa ba-niak dos-nia?

tiga kali sehari	3 times a day
tee-ga ka-li sê-ha-ree	
sebelum/selepas makan	before/after a meal
sê-bê-lum/sê-lê-pas ma-kan	
sewaktu makan	with a meal
sê-wak-too ma-kan	

Injury

. . . .

I have broken...	**Saya patah...**
	sa-ya pa-tah...
my foot	**kaki saya**
	ka-kee sa-ya
my ankle	**bukulali saya**
	boo-koo-la-lee sa-ya
my hand	**tangan saya**
	ta-ngan sa-ya

my arm	**lengan saya**
	lê-ngan sa-ya
It hurts	**Rasa sakit**
	ra-sa sa-kit

Doctor

hospital hos-pee-tal	hospital
bahagian kecederaan	casualty department
ba-ha-gee-yan	
kê-chê-dê-ra-an	
preskripsi pres-kreep-see	prescription
ambulan am-boo-lan	ambulance

FACE TO FACE

A **Saya rasa tak sedap badan**
sa-ya ra-sa tak sê-dap ba-dan
I don't feel right

B **Anda demam?**
an-da dê-mam?
Do you have a temperature?

A **Tidak/Ya, saya sakit di sini**
tee-dak/ya, sa-ya sa-kit dee see-nee
No/Yes, I have a pain here

I need to see a doctor	**Saya perlu jumpa doktor** sa-ya pêr-loo joom-pa dok-tor
My son/daughter is ill	**Anak lelaki/perempuan saya sakit** ah-nak lê-la-kee/pê-rêm-poo-wan sa-ya sa-kit
Will he/she have to go to hospital?	**Dia perlu pergi ke hospital?** dee-ya pêr-loo pêr-gee kê hos-pee-tal?
I'm on the pill	**Saya mengambil pil perancang** sa-ya mêng-am-bil pil pê-ran-chang
I'm diabetic	**Saya menghidap kencing manis** sa-ya mêng-hee-dap kên-ching ma-nis
I need insulin	**Saya perlukan insulin** sa-ya pêr-loo-kan in-soo-lin
I'm allergic to penicillin	**Saya alah kepada penisilin** sa-ya ah-lah kê-pa-da pe-ni-si-lin
Will I have to pay?	**Saya perlu bayar?** sa-ya pêr-loo ba-yar?
Can you give me a receipt for the insurance?	**Boleh anda berikan saya resit untuk insuran?** bo-leh an-da bê-ree-kan sa-ya reh-sit oon-tuk in-soo-ran?

Dentist

•••••••••••••••••••••••••••••••••••••

Look out for signs saying '**Klinik Gigi**' or '**Klinik Pergigian**' (dental clinic) or '**Doktor Gigi**' (dentist). Be sure to ask for a receipt for insurance purposes.

tampalan	tam-pa-lan	filling
korona	ko-ro-na	crown
gigi palsu	gee-gee pal-soo	dentures
suntikan	soon-ti-kan	injection

I need to go to a dentist	**Saya perlu jumpa doktor gigi** sa-ya per-loo joom-pa dok-tor gee-gee
He/she has toothache	**Dia sakit gigi** dee-ya sa-kit gee-gee
This hurts	**Sakit sini** sa-kit see-ni
My filling has come out	**Tampalan saya tertanggal** tam-pa-lan sa-ya têr-tang-gal
My crown has come out	**Korona saya tertanggal** ko-ro-na sa-ya têr-tang-gal
Can you do emergency treatment?	**Boleh anda beri rawatan kecemasan?** bo-leh an-da bê-ree ra-wa-tan kê-chê-ma-san?

Different types of travellers

Disabled travellers

. . . .

Is there a toilet for the disabled?	**Ada tak tandas untuk orang kurang upaya?**
	ah-da tak tan-das oon-tuk oh-rang koo-rang oo-pa-ya?
I want a room on the ground floor	**Saya hendak bilik di tingkat bawah**
	saya hên-dak bee-lik dee ting-kat ba-wah
Can I visit in a wheelchair?	**Boleh saya melawat dengan kerusi roda?**
	bo-leh sa-ya mê-la-wat dê-ngan kê-roo-see ro-da?
Is there a lift?	**Ada tak lif?**
	ah-da tak lif?
Is there a reduction for the disabled?	**Ada tak diskaun untuk orang kurang-upaya?**
	ah-da tak dis-kaun oon-tuk oh-rang koo-rang oo-pa-ya?
I am deaf	**Saya cacat pendengaran**
	sa-ya cha-chat pên-dê-nga-ran

> **Hotel (booking)** (p 52) > **Hotel desk** (p 55)

With kids

A child's ticket	**Tiket kanak-kanak**
	tee-ket ka-nak-ka-nak
He/she is ... years old	**Dia berumur ... tahun**
	dee-ya bêr-oo-moor ... ta-hoon
Is there a reduction for children?	**Ada tak diskaun untuk kanak-kanak?**
	ah-da tak dis-kaun oon-tuk ka-nak-ka-nak?
Do you have a children's menu?	**Ada tak menu untuk kanak-kanak?**
	ah-da tak me-noo oon-tuk ka-nak-ka-nak?
Is it OK to take children?	**Boleh tak bawa kanak-kanak?**
	bo-leh tak ba-wa ka-nak-ka-nak?
Do you have...?	**Anda ada...?**
	an-da ah-da...?
a high chair	**kerusi tinggi budak**
	kê-roo-see ting-gee boo-dak
a cot	**katil budak**
	ka-til boo-dak

Reference

Alphabet

• •

In Malay, Q and X appear mostly in words borrowed from other languages. For instance, '**qisas**' (meaning an Arabic poem) is borrowed from Arabic, while 'X-ray' is borrowed from English. The following is a list of words to use when you need to spell something out in Malay:

How do you spell it?	**Bagaimana hendak mengejanya?**
	ba-gai-ma-na hên-dak mê-nge-ja-nia?
A like 'aku'	**A macam 'aku'**
	a ma-cham 'ah-koo'
B like 'bas'	**B macam 'bas'**
	b ma-cham 'bas'

A	a	**Aku**	ah-koo
B	b	**Bas**	bas
C	c	**Cantik**	chan-tik
D	d	**Dalam**	da-lam
E	e	**Ela**	eh-la
F	f	**Fikir**	fi-kir
G	g	**Gula**	goo-la
H	h	**Hari**	ha-ree
I	i	**Ilmu**	il-moo
J	j	**Jala**	ja-la
K	k	**Kapas**	ka-pas
L	l	**Lalat**	la-lat
M	m	**Masin**	ma-sin
N	n	**Nasi**	na-see
O	o	**Orang**	oh-rang
P	p	**Patah**	pa-tah
Q	q	**Qada**	qa-da
R	r	**Rabu**	ra-boo
S	s	**Saya**	sa-ya
T	t	**Tali**	ta-lee
U	u	**Ular**	oo-lar
V	v	**Van**	van
W	w	**Wakil**	wa-kil
X	x	**X-ray**	x-ray
Y	y	**Yakin**	ya-kin
Z	z	**Zaitun**	zai-toon

Alphabet

Measurements and quantities

•••

Liquids

half a litre of...	**setengah liter...** sê-tê-ngah lee-têr...
one litre of...	**satu liter...** sa-too lee-têr...
2 litres of...	**dua liter...** doo-wa lee-têr...
a bottle of...	**sebotol...** sê-bo-tol...
a glass of...	**segelas...** sê-gê-las...

Weights

100 grams of...	**seratus gram...** sê-ra-tus gram...
half a kilo of...	**setengah kilo...** sê-tê-ngah kee-lo...
one kilo of...	**sekilo...** sê-kee-lo...
two kilos of...	**dua kilo...** doo-wa kee-lo...

Food

a slice of...	**sepotong...**
	sê-po-tong...
a dozen	**sedozen**
	sê-do-zen
a box of...	**sekotak...**
	sê-ko-tak...
a carton of...	**sekartun...**
	sê-kar-toon...

Miscellaneous

double	**dua kali ganda**
	doo-wa ka-lee gan-da
more	**lebih**
	lê-bih
less	**kurang**
	koo-rang
enough	**cukup**
	choo-kup
single	**satu**
	sa-too

Numbers

When showing amounts, Malay usually uses words called numerical classifiers, like '**biji**' for fruits, '**orang**' for people, '**ekor**' for animals and so forth. These numerical classifiers appear in between the number and the noun. For instance, 'two apples' would be '**dua biji epal**' and 'four cats' would be '**empat ekor kucing**'.

	Number	Numerical classifier	Noun
English:	two		apples
Malay:	dua	biji	epal
English:	four		cats
Malay:	empat	ekor	kucing

English has similar words, too, as in 'a **bag** of rubbish', 'a **bowl** of noodles', or 'a **piece** of furniture'.

0	**kosong** ko-song
1	**satu** sa-too
2	**dua** doo-wa
3	**tiga** tee-ga
4	**empat** êm-pat

5	**lima** lee-ma	
6	**enam** ê-nam	
7	**tujuh** too-juh	
8	**lapan** la-pan	
9	**sembilan** sêm-bee-lan	
10	**sepuluh** sê-poo-luh	
11	**sebelas** sê-bê-las	
12	**dua belas** doo-wa bê-las	
13	**tiga belas** tee-ga bê-las	
14	**empat belas** êm-pat bê-las	
15	**lima belas** lee-ma bê-las	
16	**enam belas** ê-nam bê-las	
17	**tujuh belas** too-juh bê-las	
18	**lapan belas** la-pan bê-las	
19	**sembilan belas** sêm-bee-lan bê-las	
20	**dua-puluh** doo-wa-poo-luh	
30	**tiga-puluh** tee-ga-poo-luh	
40	**empat-puluh** êm-pat-poo-luh	
50	**lima-puluh** lee-ma-poo-luh	
60	**enam puluh** ê-nam-poo-luh	
70	**tujuh puluh** too-juh-poo-luh	
80	**lapan puluh** la-pan-poo-luh	
90	**sembilan puluh** sêm-bee-lan-poo-luh	
100	**seratus** sê-ra-tus	
200	**dua ratus** doo-wa ra-tus	
300	**tiga ratus** tee-ga ra-tus	
400	**empat ratus** êm-pat ra-tus	
500	**lima ratus** lee-ma ra-tus	

Numbers

1000	**seribu** sê-ree-boo
2000	**dua ribu** doo-wa ree-boo
3000	**tiga ribu** tee-ga ree-boo
10,000	**sepuluh ribu** sê-poo-luh ree-boo
100,000	**seratus ribu** sê-ra-tus ree-boo
1,000,000	**sejuta** sê-joo-ta

first	**pertama** pêr-ta-ma
second	**kedua** kê-doo-wa
third	**ketiga** kê-tee-ga
fourth	**keempat** kê-êm-pat
fifth	**kelima** kê-lee-ma
sixth	**keenam** kê-ê-nam
seventh	**ketujuh** kê-too-juh
eighth	**kelapan** kê-la-pan
ninth	**kesembilan** kê-sêm-bee-lan
tenth	**kesepuluh** kê-sê-poo-luh

Days and months

Days

Monday	**Isnin**	is-nin
Tuesday	**Selasa**	sê-la-sa
Wednesday	**Rabu**	ra-boo
Thursday	**Khamis**	kha-mis
Friday	**Jumaat**	joo-ma-at
Saturday	**Sabtu**	sab-too
Sunday	**Ahad**	ah-had
weekend	**Hari minggu**	ha-ree ming-goo

Months

January	**Januari**	ja-noo-wa-ree
February	**Febuari**	fe-boo-wa-ree
March	**Mac**	mach
April	**April**	ah-pril
May	**Mei**	mey
June	**Jun**	joon
July	**Julai**	Joo-lai
August	**Ogos**	o-gos
September	**September**	sep-tem-bêr
October	**Oktober**	ok-to-bêr
November	**November**	no-vem-bêr
December	**Disember**	dee-sem-bêr

Seasons

Malaysia is warm and very humid throughout the year. Rain is often accompanied by thunder and lightning, and may last an hour or more. There are two distinct seasons: **the dry season** from May to September and **the rainy season** from mid-November until March.

Time

Malaysia uses the 24-hour clock and Malaysian standard time is 8 hours ahead of Greenwich Mean Time (GMT +8).

am (morning)	**pagi**
	pa-gee
It's midday	**Sudah tengahari**
	soo-dah tê-nga-ha-ree
pm (afternoon)	**tengahari**
	tê-nga-ha-ree
It's...	**Sudah...**
	soo-dah...
It's 1 o'clock (afternoon)	**Sudah pukul satu (tengahari)**
	soo-dah poo-kul sa-too (tê-nga-ha-ree)

It's 2 o'clock (afternoon)	**Sudah pukul dua (petang)** soo-dah poo-kul doo-wa (pê-tang)
What time is it?	**Pukul berapa sekarang?** poo-kul bê-ra-pa sê-ka-rang?
9.00	**sembilan** sêm-bee-lan
9.10	**sembilan sepuluh minit** sêm-bee-lan sê-poo-luh mi-nit
9.15	**sembilan suku** sêm-bee-lan soo-koo
9.30	**sembilan setengah** sêm-bee-lan sê-tê-ngah
9.45	**sembilan empat-puluh lima** sêm-bee-lan êm-pat poo-luh lee-ma
9.50	**sembilan lima-puluh** sêm-bee-lan lee-ma poo-luh
What is the date?	**Apa tarikh hari ini?** ah-pa ta-rikh ha-ree ee-nee?
It's 16 September 2006	**Hari ini enam belas September dua ribu enam** ha-ree ee-nee ê-nam bê-las sep-tem-bêr doo-wa ree-boo ê-nam
today	**hari ini** ha-ree ee-nee
tomorrow	**esok** eh-sok
yesterday	**semalam** sê-ma-lam

Time

Time phrases

....

When does it begin?	**Bilakah ia akan bermula?**
	bee-la-kah ee-ya ah-kan bêr-moo-la?
When does it finish?	**Bilakah ia akan tamat?**
	bee-la-kah ee-ya ah-kan ta-mat?
When does it open?	**Bilakah ia akan dibuka?**
	bee-la-kah ee-ya ah-kan dee-boo-ka?
When does it close?	**Bilakah ia akan ditutup?**
	bee-la-kah ee-ya ah-kan dee-too-tup?
When does it leave?	**Bilakah ia akan berlepas?**
	bee-la-kah ee-ya ah-kan bêr-lê-pas?
When does it return?	**Bilakah ia akan kembali?**
	bee-la-kah ee-ya ah-kan kêm-ba-lee?
at 3 o'clock (afternoon)	**pada pukul tiga (petang)**
	pa-da poo-kul tee-ga (pê-tang)
before 3 o'clock (afternoon)	**sebelum pukul tiga (petang)**
	sê-bê-lum poo-kul tee-ga (pê-tang)
after 3 o'clock (afternoon)	**selepas pukul tiga (petang)**
	sê-lê-pas poo-kul tee-ga (pê-tang)
in the morning	**pada waktu pagi**
	pa-da wak-too pa-gee

this morning	**pagi ini**
	pa-gee ee-nee
in the afternoon	**pada waktu petang**
(until dusk)	pa-da wak-too pê-tang
in the evening	**pada waktu malam**
(after dusk)	pa-da wak-too ma-lam
in an hour's time	**dalam masa sejam**
	da-lam ma-sa sê-jam

Eating out

Eating places

Malaysia offers a mindblowing variety of dishes and 24-hour food outlets are common, especially in big cities. You will find local and international restaurants, but foodcourts are also popular, especially in shopping malls. These foodcourts have different vendors selling more affordable local dishes as well as fast food. You will find crowds of people eating at roadside food stalls, which sell food ranging from local cakes to heavier meals.

ESTABLISHMENTS	TYPE OF FOOD SERVED
gerai/warung gê-rai/wa-rung	wide variety of rice, noodles, soups and desserts
medan selera me-dan sê-le-ra	wide variety of food vendors selling all kinds of dishes

restoran cina res-toh-ran chee-na	Chinese food
restoran melayu res-toh-ran mê-la-yoo	Malay food
kafe ka-fey	Malaysian and western food, gourmet coffee and tea
restoran makanan laut res-toh-ran ma-ka-nan la-wut	specializes in seafood dishes
restoran hotel res-toh-ran hote	variety of international cuisine and may have live music
kelab malam/pab kê-lab ma-lam/pab	variety of foods and alcohol and has live music
karaoke ka-ra-oh-kay	variety of foods and has karaoke

In a bar/café

• •

Cold fruit juices made from local fruits like watermelon and lime are popular in Malaysia, while coconut water is widely known for its cooling effect. Gourmet coffee and tea can be found in most restaurants and cafés. A popular hot beverage is called **'teh tarik'** (pulled tea), which is hot tea sweetened with condensed milk. It is made by pouring the tea from a container held above head level into a container held low. You will find alcohol mostly in non-Muslim restaurants, nightclubs and hotels.

What would you like?	**Nak makan apa?** nak ma-kan ah-pa?
Hot coffee, please	**Tolong berikan saya kopi panas** toh-long bê-ree-kan sa-ya ko-pee pa-nas
Hot tea, please	**Tolong berikan saya teh panas** toh-long bê-ree-kan sa-ya teh pa-nas
A ... please	**Tolong berikan saya satu...** toh-long bê-ree-kan sa-ya sa-too...
2 ... please	**Tolong berikan saya dua...** toh-long bê-ree-kan sa-ya doo-wa...

3 ... please	**Tolong berikan saya tiga...**
	toh-long bê-ree-kan sa-ya tee-ga...
Do you have...?	**Anda ada...?**
	an-da ah-da...?
Do you have beer?	**Anda ada bir?**
	an-da ah-da bir?
Do you have brandy?	**Anda ada brandi?**
	an-da ah-da bran-dee?
a bottle of sparkling water	**sebotol air berkarbonat**
	sê-bo-tol ah-yer bêr-kar-bo-nat
sparkling mineral water	**air mineral berkarbonat**
	ah-yer mee-nê-ral bêr-kar-bo-nat
still mineral water	**air mineral tanpa karbonat**
	ah-yer mee-nê-ral tan-pa kar-bo-nat
A cappuccino, please	**Tolong berikan saya kapucino**
	toh-long bê-ree-kan sa-ya ka-poo-chee-no
A tea, please	**Tolong berikan saya teh**
	toh-long bê-ree-kan sa-ya teh
with milk	**dengan susu**
	dê-ngan soo-soo
with lemon	**dengan limau**
	dê-ngan lee-mau
with ice	**dengan ais**
	dê-ngan ais
with sugar	**dengan gula**
	dê-ngan goo-la

without sugar	**tanpa gula**
	tan-pa goo-la
one more, please	**tolong berikan saya satu lagi**
	toh-long bê-ree-kan sa-ya sa-too
	la-gee

Reading the menu

Most Malaysians do not eat multi-course meals, and you will find detailed menus only in the bigger restaurants and cafés. Rice is a staple food in Malaysia, and it is usually served with a variety of meat, poultry, seafood or vegetable side dishes called **lauk** (la-wuk). Lauk can be rich and spicy, like curry, or light and mild, like soup. There are also different types of fried rice and noodle dishes. Malaysian desserts are usually rich and sweet, but fruit is quite popular too. Breads are not considered as staple food, but the favourite **roti canai** (roh-tee cha-nai) or puffed bread is widely eaten, especially for breakfast. Tipping is not customary, but you can do so at your discretion. Hotels and bigger restaurants will add a 10% service charge and a 5% government tax.

menu me-noo	menu
pembuka selera pêm-boo-ka sê-le-ra	appetizers
kerabu kê-ra-boo	spicy salad
nasi na-see	rice
tumis too-mis	stir-fried in oil until aromatic
sup soop	soup
kari ka-ree	curry
sambal sam-bal	red chilli gravy
pencuci mulut pên-choo-chee moo-lut	dessert

In a restaurant

The menu, please	**Tolong berikan saya menu** toh-long bê-ree-kan sa-ya me-noo
Is there a set menu?	**Ada tak menu tetap?** ah-da tak me-noo tê-tap?
What is this?	**Apa ini?** ah-pa ee-nee?
I'd like this	**Saya mahu yang ini** sa-ya ma-hoo yang ee-nee

What is the speciality of the house?	**Apakah hidangan istimewa di sini?** ah-pa-kah hee-da-ngan is-tee-me-wa dee see-nee?
Excuse me!	**Maafkan saya!** ma-af-kan sa-ya!
The bill, please	**Tolong berikan saya bil** toh-long bê-ree-kan sa-ya bil
Some more rice, please	**Tolong berikan saya nasi lagi** toh-long bê-ree-kan sa-ya na-see la-gee
Some more water, please	**Tolong berikan saya air lagi** toh-long bê-ree-kan sa-ya ah-yer la-gee
salt	**garam** ga-ram
pepper	**lada hitam** la-da hee-tam
Another bottle, please	**Tolong berikan saya sebotol lagi** toh-long bê-ree-kan sa-ya sê-bo-tol la-gee
Another glass, please	**Tolong berikan saya segelas lagi** toh-long bê-ree-kan sa-ya sê-gê-las la-gee

Vegetarian

· ·

If you have a hard time finding a specialist
vegetarian restaurant, try your luck at Indian
restaurants. There you may find a good variety of
Indian vegetarian food. Some bigger supermarkets
may sell imported alternative beef/chicken
products made of tofu and vegetables.

I am vegetarian	**Saya vegetarian**
	sa-ya ve-jee-ta-ri-yan
I don't eat meat	**Saya tak makan daging**
	sa-ya tak ma-kan da-ging
Is there meat in this?	**Ada tak daging dalam ini?**
	ah-da tak da-ging da-lam ee-nee?
What is there without meat?	**Ada tak hidangan tanpa daging?**
	ah-da tak hee-da-ngan tan-pa da-ging?

Vegetarian dishes

· ·

tauhu goreng/sumbat tau-hoo go-reng/soom-bat
 fried/stuffed beancurd
rojak buah ro-jak boo-wah spicy fruit and
 vegetable salad with peanut sauce
popiah sayur po-pi-yah sa-yur vegetable spring
 rolls

135

vadai va-dai potato-based patty

dosai doh-sai crepe made from rice and lentils

chapati cha-pa-tee bread made of atta flour

dalca sayur dal-cha sa-yur vegetable lentil curry

sup sayur soop sa-yur vegetable soup

pakora pa-ko-ra deep-fried vegetables dipped in batter

putu mayam poo-too ma-yam rice noodles served with coconut and brown sugar

sanwich sayur san-wich sa-yur vegetable sandwich

tempeh goreng tem-peh go-reng fried soybean cakes dipped in batter

tauhu jepun tau-hoo jê-pun fried japanese tofu with mushrooms and oyster sauce

Wines and spirits

Alcohol is usually served at non-Muslim restaurants, nightclubs and hotels.

The wine list, please	**Tolong berikan saya senarai wain** toh-long bê-ree-kan sa-ya sê-na-rai wain

Can you recommend a good wine?	**Boleh anda syorkan wain yang bagus?**
	bo-leh an-da shor-kan wain yang ba-gus?
A bottle of...	**Sebotol...**
	sê-bo-tol...
red wine	**wain merah**
	wain me-rah
white wine	**wain putih**
	wain poo-tih
A glass of...	**Segelas...**
	sê-gê-las...
a dry wine	**wain kering**
	wain kê-ring
a local wine	**wain tempatan**
	wain têm-pa-tan
a sweet wine	**wain manis**
	wain ma-nis

Common dishes

• •

Appetizers

Cucur udang choo-chur oo-dang prawn fritters
Karipap ka-ree-pap puff pastry filled with curried chicken or beef and potato

Keropok kê-ro-pok fried seafood or vegetable crackers

Murtabak moor-ta-bak meat and egg turnover

Pasembor pa-sem-bor fruit salad with peanut sauce

Pau pau steamed bun with sweet or mildly spicy filling

Popiah po-pi-yah spring rolls

Rojak buah ro-jak boo-wah spicy fruit and vegetable salad with peanut sauce

Roti jala ro-tee ja-la lacy crepes eaten with curry

Satay sa-tay chicken, beef or tripe kebabs

Tauhu sumbat tau-hoo soom-bat stuffed fried beancurd

Yong tau-foo yong-tau-foo variety of steamed seafood and vegetables with bean sauce

Salad

acar ah-char spicy pickled salad

kerabu betik kê-ra-boo bê-tik papaya salad

kerabu ikan kê-ra-boo ee-kan fish salad

kerabu jantung pisang kê-ra-boo jan-tung pee-sang banana flower salad

kerabu mangga kê-ra-boo mang-ga mango salad

kerabu perut kê-ra-boo pê-rut tripe salad

kerabu sotong kê-ra-boo so-tong calamari salad

kerabu suhun kê-ra-boo soo-hoon vermicelli salad

umai udang oo-mai oo-dang prawn salad

Soup

sup ayam soop ah-yam chicken soup
sup campur soop cham-pur mixed beef, chicken and seafood soup
sup daging soop da-ging beef soup
tomyam tom-yam Thai-style spicy soup with chicken/beef/seafood

Meat

ayam ah-yam chicken
babi ba-bee pork
daging da-ging beef
itik ee-tik duck

Fish and seafood

ikan air tawar ee-kan ah-yer ta-war freshwater fish
ikan haruan ee-kan ha-roo-wan serpenthead
ikan keli ee-kan kê-lee catfish
ikan laut ee-kan la-wut saltwater fish
kerang kê-rang mussels
ketam kê-tam crab
sotong so-tong squid
udang oo-dang prawns
udang karang oo-dang ka-rang lobster

Desserts

agar-agar ah-gar ah-gar sweet multicoloured jelly
ais kacang ais ka-chang milky, shaved ice dessert
cendol chen-dol coconut ice
kuih koo-wih variety of sweet local cakes
pengat pê-ngat fruit cooked in sweet coconut milk

Menu reader

acar buah ah-char boo-wah mixed pickled fruits
(sometimes spicy)

air kelapa muda ah-yer kê-la-pa moo-da fresh
coconut juice

air limau nipis ah-ye lee-mau nee-pis lime juice

air mata kucing ah-yer ma-ta koo-ching longan
juice

air laici ah-yer lai-chee lychee juice

air mineral ah-yer mee-nê-ral mineral water

air minuman ah-yer mee-noo-man drinking water

ais ais ice

ais kosong ais ko-song plain iced water

anggur ang-goor grapes

asam pedas daging ah-sam pê-das da-ging beef
in spice tamarind gravy

asparagus goreng belacan as-pa-ra-gus go-reng
bê-la-chan asparagus stir-fried in prawn paste

ayam berkicap ah-yam bêr-kee-chap stir-fried
chicken with soy sauce

ayam gajus ah-yam ga-jus stir-fried chicken with
cashew nuts and dried chilli

ayam golek ah-yam go-lek roasted chicken

ayam masak merah ah-yam ma-sak me-rah chicken with tomato and chilli paste

ayam tandoori ah-yam tan-doo-ree chicken baked in clay oven

bergedil bêr-gê-dil beef and potato patty

bir beer beer

brandi bran-dee brandy

buah boo-wah fruit

buah delima boo-wah dê-lee-ma pomegranate

buah laici boo-wah lai-chee lychee

buah mata kucing bu-wah ma-ta koo-ching longan

buah nona boo-wah no-na custard apple

bubur nasi boo-bur na-see rice porridge

chee chong fun chee chong farn steamed rice rolls eaten with sauces

cili api chi-lee ah-pee chilli peppers (extremely hot)

cili jeruk chi-lee jê-ruk pickled chillies

cucur udang choo-chur oo-dang prawn fritters

daging babi da-ging ba-bee ham

daging goreng berkunyit da-ging go-reng bêr-koo-nyit beef stir-fried in turmeric

daging lada hitam da-ging la-da hee-tam black pepper beef

daun salad da-wun sa-lad lettuce

durian doo-ri-yan durian

epal eh-pal apple

garam ga-ram salt
...goreng go-reng fried...
gula goo-la sugar

ikan ee-kan fish
ikan bakar ee-kan bakar grilled fish
ikan bawal kukus ee-kan ba-wal koo-kus steamed pomfret
ikan bilis goreng berlada ee-kan bee-lis go-reng bêr-la-da anchovies fried with red chillies and peanuts
ikan keli ee-kan kê-lee catfish
ikan kerapu masam manis ee-kan kê-ra-poo ma-sam ma-nis grouper fish in sweet and sour sauce
ikan masin ee-kan ma-sin salted fish
ikan pari bakar ee-kan pa-ree ba-kar BBQ stingray marinated in spices
ikan siakap kukus ee-kan see-ya-kap koo-kus steamed sea bass

jem jem jam
jus epal jus eh-pal apple juice
jus mangga jus mang-g mango juice
jus nenas jus nê-nas pineapple juice

jus oren jus oh-ren orange juice

jus tembikai jus têm-bee-kai watermelon juice

jus tomato jus to-ma-to tomato juice

kangkung goreng belacan kang-kung go-reng bê-la-chan kangkung vegetable stir-fried with prawn paste

kailan goreng ikan masin kai-lan go-reng ee-kan ma-sin Chinese kale stir-fried with salted fish

kailan sos tiram kai-lan sos tee-ram Chinese kale stir-fried in oyster sauce

kari ka-ree (ah-yam, da-ging, ee-kan) spicy curry (chicken, beef or fish)

kari kepala ikan ka-ree kê-pa-la ee-kan fish-head curry

kaya ka-ya sweet spread made of sugar and coconut milk

keju keh-joo cheese

kerabu kê-ra-boo spicy salads

kerabu taugeh kê-ra-boo tau-geh bean sprouts salad

kerabu telur rebus kê-ra-boo tê-lur rê-bus boiled egg salad

kerang bakar kê-rang ba-kar BBQ mussels

kerang rebus kê-rang rê-bus boiled mussels

ketam kê-tam crab

ketam bercili kê-tam bêr-chee-lee chilli crabs

ketam masam manis kê-tam ma-sam ma-nis sweet and sour crabs

kentang lenyek kên-tang le-nyek mashed potato

kicap manis kee-chap ma-nis sweet soy sauce

kicap masin kee-chap ma-sin salty soy sauce

koay teow goreng kway tee-yow go-reng fried flat rice noodles

kobis ko-bis cabbage

kopi o ais ko-pee oh ais iced black coffee

kopi panas ko-pee pa-nas hot coffee

kopi segera ko-pee sê-gê-ra instant coffee

kuih keria koo-wih kê-ree-ya sweet potato doughnuts

kurma kambing koor-ma kam-bing mutton korma

lada benggala la-da bêng-ga-la bell peppers

lada hitam la-da hee-tam black pepper

laksa lak-sa noodles in tangy fish soup

limau barli lee-mau bar-lee pomelo

limau manis lee-mau ma-nis tangerine

madu ma-doo honey

masak lemak ketam ma-sak lê-mak kê-tam crab cooked in coconut milk and turmeric

masak lemak telur itik ma-sak lê-mak tê-lur ee-tik duck eggs cooked in coconut milk and turmeric

mee goreng mamak mee go-reng ma-mak spicy fried yellow noodles

mee hoon goreng mee-hoon go-reng fried vermicelli

mee jawa mee ja-wa garnished yellow noodles with prawn gravy

mee kungfu mee koong-foo crispy Chinese rice noodles in gravy

mee rebus mee rê-boos garnished yellow noodles in thick gravy

mee udang mee oo-dang prawn noodles

mee wonton mee won-ton thin egg noodles garnished with dumplings

minyak zaitun mee-niak zai-toon olive oil

nasi ayam na-see ah-yam rice cooked in chicken stock

nasi biryani na-see bir-ya-nee rice sauteed in ghee and cooked in saffron

nasi campur na-see cham-pur white rice served with a variety of side dishes

nasi goreng cina na-see go-reng chee-na fried rice with chicken/meat/seafood and mixed vegetables

nasi goreng kampung na-see go-reng kam-poong fried rice with anchovies

nasi kerabu na-see kê-ra-boo rice served with herbs, grated coconut, shredded fish and gravy

nasi lemak na-see lê-mak rice cooked in coconut milk

nasi tomato na-see to-ma-to rice cooked in
   tomato sauce/puree
nenas nê-nas pineapple
nuget ayam na-get ah-yam chicken nuggets

oren oh-ren orange
otak-otak oh-tak oh-tak steamed or grilled fish
   mousse

pecal pê-chal steamed vegetables with spicy sauce
penkek pen-kek pancake

rambutan ram-boo-tan rambutan
rebung rê-bung young bamboo shoot
rendang daging rên-dang da-ging spiced beef
   simmered in coconut milk
restoran res-toh-ran restaurant
roti canai ro-tee cha-nai traditional puffed
   flatbread

salad sa-lad salad
sambal belacan sam-bal bê-la-chan pounded hot
   chillies with prawn paste
sambal tumis sam-bal too-mis aromatic red chilli
   gravy stir-fried in oil
sambal udang sam-bal oo-dang prawn stir-fried in
   spicy sambal gravy

sandwic tuna san-wich too-na tuna sandwich

sayur campur cina sa-yur cham-pur chee-na
Chinese-style stir-fried mixed vegetables

sayur goreng sa-yur go-reng stir-fried vegetables

sayur lodeh sa-yur lo-deh vegetables stewed in
coconut gravy and served with rice cubes

sos cili sos chee-lee chilli sauce

sos tomato sos to-ma-to tomato ketchup

soto so-to spicy chicken soup garnished and eaten
with rice cubes or noodles

sotong so-tong calamari/squid

sotong celup tepung so-tong che-lup tê-pung
deep-fried battered calamari

stek stek steak

stroberi stro-be-ree strawberry

sup soop soup

sup bebola ikan sup bê-bo-la ee-kan fishball soup

sup cendawan soop chen-da-wan mushroom
soup

sup ekor soop eh-kor oxtail soup

sup kambing soop kam-bing aromatic mutton
soup

sup sawi soop sa-wi mustard greens soup

sup tauhu soop tau-hoo tofu soup

tauchu tau-choo black bean sauce

taugeh goreng tau-geh go-reng stir-fried bean
sprouts

teh halia teh ha-lee-ya ginger tea

teh o ais teh oh ais iced black tea
teh o ais limau teh oh ais lee-mau iced lemon tea
teh panas teh pa-nas hot tea with creamer
telur asin tê-lur ah-sin salted eggs
telur bungkus tê-lur boong-kus minced meat or
  chicken wrapped with egg
telur rebus tê-lur rê-bus boiled eggs
tembikai têm-bee-kai watermelon
timun tee-moon cucumber

udang bakar oo-dang ba-kar grilled prawns
udang karang oo-dang ka-rang lobster
udang masak lemak oo-dang ma-sak lê-mak
  prawns cooked in turmeric and coconut milk
udang mentega oo-dang mên-te-ga butter
  prawns

wiski wis-kee whisky

Grammar

Sentence structure

••••••••••••••••••••••••••••••••••••••

Malay sentences are arranged according to subject + verb + object, like English. Words are commonly formed by attaching prefixes and suffixes to root words. For example, if the root word is **'hijau'** (hee-jau) or 'green', you can form the Malay word for 'greenish' simply by adding 'ke' as a prefix and 'an' as a suffix.

green   **hijau** (hee-jau)
greenish   **kehijauan** (kê-hee-jau-an)

Malay also borrows words from a variety of languages, like English, Arabic, Portuguese and Sanskrit.

Pronouns

In Malay, you will not be able to tell a person's gender by the pronoun used, and unlike English, Malay pronouns appear after nouns. For instance, in English you would say, 'my face', whereas in Malay, you would say '**muka** (face) **saya** (my)'.

The most frequently used Malay pronouns are explained below:

I/me	**Saya** (sa-ya): Suitable for formal and informal situations, is considered most polite.
	Aku (ah-koo) : Used among close friends and equals, and is not recommended when speaking with elders or in formal situations.
You	**Anda** (an-da): This is considered most polite and is used in formal situations and correspondence.
	Awak/Kamu/Engkau/Kau (ah-wak/ka-moo/êng-kau/kau): Used among close friends and equals.
We/us	**Kami** (ka-mee): Used when speaking to a third party about yourself and your companion(s)

	Kita (kee-ta): Used when you are speaking with your companion(s) about yourself.	
He/him/ she/her	**Dia** (dee-ya)	
	Beliau (bê-lee-yau): Used when speaking about someone with respect, usually an important person or an elderly person.	
They/them	**Mereka** (mê-re-ka)	
It	**Ia** (ee-ya): Refers to non-human subjects.	

Verbs

• •

Malay verbs do not change for different tenses, plurals or gender, and there are no articles (a, an, the). Tense is indicated by context or specific words that show time, as explained below:

'**sedang**' (sê-dang) and '**masih**' (ma-sih) indicate the present time.

'**akan**' (ah-kan) and '**nanti**' (nan-tee) indicate the future.

'**telah**' (tê-lah), '**sudah**' (soo-dah) and '**pernah**' (pêr-nah) indicate the past.

In the following examples, the verb is '**pergi**' (to go).

Present continuous tense

She is going to Kuala Lumpur

Dia sedang pergi ke Kuala Lumpur
dee-ya sê-dang pêr-gee kê koo-wa-la loom-pur

Future tense

She will go to Kuala Lumpur next week

Dia akan pergi ke Kuala Lumpur pada minggu depan
dee-ya akan pêr-gee kê koo-wa-la loom-pur pa-da ming-goo dê-pan

Past tense

She went to Kuala Lumpur yesterday

Dia telah pergi ke Kuala Lumpur semalam
dee-ya tê-lah pêr-gee kê koo-wa-la loom-pur sê-ma-lam

Adjectives

In Malay, the adjective follows the noun. In the following example, the adjective is '**indah**' (beautiful) and the noun is '**negara**' (country):

Malaysia is a beautiful country	**Malaysia negara yang indah**
	ma-lay-see-ya nê-ga-ra yang een-dah

Negatives

The words '**bukan**' and '**tidak**' are used in a negative sentence. '**Bukan**' is mostly used with nouns and pronouns, and '**tidak**' is mostly used with verbs and adjectives.

I am hungry	**Saya lapar**
	sa-ya la-par
I am not hungry	**Saya tidak lapar**
	sa-ya tee-dak la-par
She wants to go out	**Dia hendak keluar**
	dee-ya hên-dak kê-loo-war

She doesn't want to go out	**Dia tidak hendak keluar**
	dee-ya tee-dak hên-dak kê-loo-war
He is the leader	**Dia ketua**
	dee-ya kê-too-wa
He is not the leader	**Dia bukan ketua**
	dee-ya boo-kan kê-too-wa
She is a swimmer	**Dia perenang**
	dee-ya pê-rê-nang
She is not a swimmer	**Dia bukan perenang**
	dee-ya boo-kan pê-rê-nang

Questions

You can change a statement into a question by using the following interrogatives:

what	**apa** ah-pa
when	**bila** bee-la
where	**di mana** dee ma-na
why	**kenapa/mengapa**
	kê-na-pa/mê-nga-pa
how	**bagaimana** ba-gai-ma-na
who/whom	**siapa** see-ya-pa
how many	**berapa** bê-ra-pa

For example:

Statement

She went home.

Dia pulang ke rumah
dee-ya poo-lang kê roo-mah

Question

When did she go home?

Bila dia pulang ke rumah?
bee-la dee-ya poo-lang kê roo-mah?

Prepositions

about	**tentang** tên-tang
from	**dari** da-ree
in, at	**dalam, pada** da-lam, pa-da
on	**atas** ah-tas
under	**bawah** ba-wah
by/with	**oleh/dengan** o-leh/dê-ngan
between	**antara** an-ta-ra
without	**tanpa** tan-pa
except	**kecuali** kê-choo-wa-lee
inside	**dalam** da-lam
outside	**luar** loo-war

Public holidays

••••••••••••••••••••••••••••••••••••

Malaysia has many national holidays. The main celebrations are as follows:

1 January	**New Year's Day** is celebrated on a grand scale in Kuala Lumpur with free pop concerts and firework displays.
	Awal Muharram
	ah-wal moo-ha-ram This signifies the start of the Islamic New Year. The exact date depends on the Islamic calendar, which is 11 days shorter than the solar year.
	Chinese New Year The traditional Chinese New Year celebrations last for fifteen days. The exact date is determined by the Chinese lunar calendar. Offices and schools are usually closed for two days.
1 May	**National Labour Day**
7 June	**Birthday of the Yang di-Pertuang Agong** yang dee pêr-too-wan ah-gong The official birthday of the Yang di-Pertuan

Agong of Malaysia is celebrated every year. On this day, His Majesty confers awards to honour Malaysians who have made significant contributions or service to the country.

31 August   **Merdeka day** mêr-de-ka is to commemorate Malaysia's independence from British rule in 1957. In Kuala Lumpur, people gather at Dataran Merdeka to celebrate.

Deepavali dee-pa-va-lee This is the annual Indian Festival of Lights, which is celebrated during the seventh month of the Hindu calendar. Offices and schools are usually closed for a day.

Hari Raya Aidil-Fitri ha-ree ra-ya ai-deel fee-tree Muslims celebrate Aidil-Fitri after a month of fasting. The exact date is determined by the sighting of the new moon, and offices and schools are usually closed for two days.

Hari Raya Aidil Adha

ha-ree ra-ya ai-deel ad-ha This is a Muslim celebration to commemorate the holy pilgrimage to Mecca and the sacrifices of the Prophet Abraham. Held on the tenth day of the last month in the Muslim calendar.

25 December **Christmas** Offices and schools are usually closed for a day.

A

English	Malay	Pronunciation
a(n)	satu	sa-too
about	tentang	tén-tang
above	di atas	dee ah-tas
to accept	menerima	mê-nê-ree-ma
do you accept Visa®?	anda terima Visa®?	an-da té-ree-ma Visa?
accident	kemalangan	kê-ma-la-ngan
ache	sakit	sa-kit
address	alamat	ah-la-mat
admission charge	bayaran masuk	ba-ya-ran ma-suk
adult	dewasa	de-wa-sa
aeroplane	kapalterbang	ka-pal-tér-bang
after	selepas	sê-lê-pas
afternoon	tengahari	té-nga-ha-ree
in the afternoon	pada waktu	pa-da wak-too
	tengahari	té-nga-ha-ree
this afternoon	tengahari ini	té-nga-ha-ree ee-nee
tomorrow afternoon	tengahari esok	té-nga-ha-ree eh-sok
again	sekali lagi	sê-ka-lee la-ge
age	umur	oo-mur
agent	ejen	eh-jên
estate agent	ejen hartanah	eh-jên har-ta-nah
travel agent	ejen	eh-jên pé-lan-
	pelancongan	cho-ngan
ago	dahulu	da-hoo-loo
ahead	di hadapan	dee ha-da-pan
straight ahead	terus di	té-roos dee
	hadapan	ha-da-pan
air	penghawa	pêng-ha-wa
conditioning	dingin	dee-ngin
airport	lapangan	la-pa-ngan
	terbang	tér-bang
alarm	penggera	pêng-gê-ra
alarm clock	jam penggera	jam pêng-gê-ra
alcohol	alkohol	al-ko-hol
without alcohol	tanpa alkohol	tan-pa al-ko-hol
all	semua	sê-moo-wa

English	Malay	Pronunciation
to be allergic to	alah kepada	ah-lah kê-pa-da
alright (OK)	tak apa-apa	tak apa-apa
are you all right?	anda tak apa-apa?	an-da tak ah-pa-ah-pa?
I'm all right	Saya tak apa-apa	Sa-ya tak ah-pa-ah-pa
alone	sendiri	sên-dee-ree
always	sentiasa	sên-tee-ya-sa
ambulance	ambulan	am-boo-lan
America	Amerika	Ah-me-ree-ka
American	orang Amerika	oh-rang Ah-me-ree-ka
and	dan	dan
angry	marah	ma-rah
I'm angry	Saya marah	Sa-ya-ma-rah
another	satu lagi	sa-too la-gee
another beer	satu lagi bir	sa-too la-gee bir
answer	jawapan	ja-wa-pan
there's no answer (phone)	takda jawapan	tak-da ja-wa-pan
to answer	menjawab	mên-ja-wab

English	Malay	Pronunciation
answering machine	mesin penjawab	meh-sin pên-ja-wab
ants	semut	sê-mut
any	apa saja	ah-pa saja
have you any matches?	anda ada mancis?	an-da ada man-chis?
apartment	apartmen	ah-part-mên
apple	epal	eh-pal
apple juice	jus epal	joos eh-pal
April	April	Ah-pril
arm	lengan	lê-ngan
my arm hurts	lengan saya sakit	lê-ngan sa-ya sa-kit
to arrest	menahan	mê-na-han
arrivals	ketibaan	kê-tee-ba-an
to arrive	tiba	tee-ba
art gallery	galeri lukisan	ga-lê-ree loo-kee-san
artist	pelukis	pê-loo-kis
ashtray	bekas abu rokok	bê-kas ah-boo ro-kok

English – Malay

asthma	lelah	lê-lah
at (place)	di	dee
(time)	pada	pa-da
to attack	menyerang	mê-nyê-rang
I've been attacked	Saya telah diserang	Sa-ya tê-lah dee-sê-rang
attack (verb)	serang	sê-rang
(noun)	serangan	sê-ra-ngan
heart attack	serangan jantung	sê-ra-ngan jan-tung
attention	perhatian	pêr-ha-tee-yan
attractive	menarik	mê-na-rik
August	Ogos	O-gos
aunt	makcik	mak-chik
Australia	Australia	Os-tra-lee-ya
Australian	orang Australia	oh-rang Os-tra-lee-ya
automatic car	kereta automatik	kê-re-ta oh-to-ma-tik
away	pergi	pêr-gee

| | tolong pergi dari sini! | toh-long pêr-gee da-ree see-nee! |
| please go away! | | |

B

baby	bayi	ba-yee
baby food	makanan bayi	ma-ka-nan ba-yee
babysitter	pengasuh	pê-nga-suh
back (of body)	belakang	bê-la-kang
backpack	beg galas	beg ga-las
bad	buruk	boo-ruk
bag	beg	beg
baggage	bagasi	ba-ga-see
baggage reclaim	tuntutan bagasi	tun-too-tan ba-ga-see
baker's	kedai tukang buat roti	kê-dai too-kang boo-wat ro-tee
ball	bola	bo-la
bandage	balutan	ba-lu-tan
bank	bank	benk

English	Malay	Pronunciation
where is the bank?	di manakah bank?	dee ma-na-kah benk?
bar	bar	bar
barber	tukang gunting rambut	too-kang goon-ting ram-but
bargain	menawar	mê-na-war
no bargaining	dilarang menawar	dee-la-rang mê-na-war
basket	bakul	ba-kul
bath	mandi	man-dee
bathroom	bilik mandi	bee-lik man-dee
where is the bathroom?	di manakah bilik mandi?	dee ma-na-kah bee-lik man-dee?
with bathroom	dengan bilik mandi	dê-ngan bee-lik man-dee
battery (for car)	bateri	ba-tê-ree
battery (for torch, camera)	baterinya sudah lemah	ba-tê-ree-nia soo-dah lê-mah
I need batteries for this	Saya perlukan bateri untuk ini	Sa-ya pêr-loo-kan ba-tê-ree oon-tuk ee-nee
bazaar	bazar	ba-zar
where is the bazaar?	di manakah bazar?	dee ma-na-kah ba-zar?
be	menjadi	mên-ja-dee
beach	pantai	pan-tai
how far is the beach?	berapa jauhkah pantai?	bê-ra-pa ja-wuh-kah pan-tai?
beautiful	cantik	chan-tik
bed	katil	ka-til
double bed	katil kelamin	ka-til kê-la-min
twin beds	katil kembar	ka-til kêm-bar
bedclothes	peralatan tempat tidur	pêr-ah-la-tan têm-pat tee-dur
I need more bedclothes	Saya perlukan peralatan tempat tidur lagi	Sa-ya pêr-loo-kan pêr-ah-la-tan têm-pat tee-dur la-gee
these bedclothes are dirty	peralatan tempat tidur ini kotor	pêr-ah-la-tan têm-pat tee-dur ee-nee ko-tor
bedroom	bilik tidur	bee-lik tee-dur

English – Malay

English	Malay	Pronunciation
double bedroom	bilik kelamin	bee-lik kê-la-min
single bedroom	bilik bujang	bee-lik boo-jang
bee	lebah	lê-bah
beef	daging	da-ging
beer	bir	beer
a bottle of beer	sebotol bir	sê-bo-tol beer
a glass of beer	segelas bir	sê-gê-las beer
before	sebelum	sê-bê-lum
before	sebelum	sê-bê-lum
4 o'clock	pukul 4	poo-kul êm-pat
before dinner	sebelum makan malam	sê-bê-lum ma-kan ma-lam
to begin	bermula	bêr-moo-la
behind	di belakang	dee bê-la-kang
to believe	mempercayai	mêm-pêr-cha-ya-ee
I don't believe you	Saya tak percayakan anda	Sa-ya tak per-cha-ya-kan an-da
below	di bawah	dee ba-wah
belt	tali pinggang	ta-lee ping-gang
money belt	tali pinggang duit	ta-lee ping-gang doo-wit
seat belt	tali keledar	ta-lee kê-le-dar
bend (verb)	bongkok/bengkok	bong-kok/bengkok
	selekoh	sê-le-koh
beside	di sebelah	dee sê-bê-lah
best	terbaik	têr-ba-yik
better (than)	lebih baik (daripada)	lê-bih ba-yik (da-ree-pa-da)
bicycle	basikal	ba-see-kal
big	besar	bê-sar
bigger	lebih besar	lê-bih bê-sar
biggest	terbesar	têr-bê-sar
bill	bil	bil
the bill, please	tolong berikan saya bil	toh-long bê-ree-kan sa-ya bil
there's a mistake on the bill	ada kesilapan dalam bil	ah-da kê-see-la-pan da-lam bil
bin (for rubbish)	tong	tong
bird	burung	boo-rung
birthday	hari lahir	ha-ree la-hir

English		Malay	
happy birthday!	selamat hari lahir!	boarding card	pas masuk
birthday card	kad hari lahir	boat	bot
biscuits	biskut	boat trip	perjalanan bot
a little bit	sedikit	boiled (food)	direbus
bite (insect, dog)	gigitan		(makanan)
bitter (taste)	pahit	bone	tulang
black	hitam	book	buku
blanket	selimut	to book	tempah
to bleed	berdarah	I've booked	Saya telah menempah
blind (person)	buta	booking	penempahan
blinds	bidai	bookshop	kedai buku
(on window)		boots	kasut but
blister	lecuh	boring	membosankan
blocked	tersekat	it's boring	ia membosankan
the sink is blocked	sinki tersekat	both	kedua-duanya
blood	darah	I'd like both	Saya hendak kedua-duanya
blood group	jenis darah		
blood pressure	tekanan darah		
blue	biru		

sê-la-mat ha-ree la-hir!		pas ma-suk	
kad ha-ree la-hir		bot	
bis-kut		pêr-ja-la-nan bot	
sê-di-kit		dee-rê-bus	
gee-gee-tan		(ma-ka-nan)	
pa-hit		too-lang	
hee-tam		boo-koo	
sê-lee-mut		têm-pah	
bêr-da-rah		Sa-ya tê-lah mê-nêm-pah	
boo-ta		pê-nêm-pa-han	
bee-dai		kê-dai boo-koo	
		ka-sut boot	
lê-chuh		mêm-bo-san-kan	
têr-sê-kat		ee-ya mêm-bo-san-kan	
sing-kee têr-sê-kat		kê-doo-wa-doo-wa-nia	
da-rah			
jê-nis da-rah		Sa-ya hên-dak kê-doo-wa-doo-wa-nia	
tê-ka-nan da-rah			
bee-roo			

English – Malay

English	Malay	pronunciation
bottle	botol	bo-tol
a bottle of water	sebotol air	sê-bo-tol ah-yer
a bottle of wine	sebotol wain	sê-bo-tol wain
bottle opener	pembuka botol	pêm-boo-ka bo-tol
box	kotak	ko-tak
box office	bilik tiket	bee-lik tee-ket
boy	budak lelaki	boo-dak lê-la-kee
boyfriend	teman lelaki	tê-man lê-la-kee
brandy	brandi	bran-dee
bread	roti	ro-tee
do you sell bread?	anda jual roti?	an-da joo-wal ro-tee?
some bread, please	tolong berikan saya roti	toh-long bê-ree-kan sa-ya ro-tee
to break	memecahkan	mê-mê-chah-kan
to break down (car)	rosak	ro-sak
breakfast	sarapan pagi	sa-ra-pan pa-gee
breakfast included	sarapan pagi termasuk	sa-ra-pan pa-gee têr-ma-suk sa-ra-pan pa-gee

English	Malay	pronunciation
what is there for breakfast?	apa ada untuk sarapan pagi?	ah-pa ah-da oon-tuk sa-ra-pan pa-gee?
what time is breakfast?	sarapan pagi pada pukul berapa?	sa-ra-pan pa-gee pa-da poo-kul bê-ra-pa?
to breathe	bernafas	bêr-na-fas
bring	bawa	ba-wa
what should I bring?	apa patut saya bawa?	ah-pa pa-tut sa-ya ba-wa?
British	orang British	oh-rang Bri-tish
I'm British	Saya orang British	Sa-ya oh-rang Bri-tish
brochure	risalah	ree-sa-lah
have you got a brochure in English?	anda ada risalah dalam bahasa Inggeris?	an-da ah-da ree-sa-lah da-lam ba-ha-sa Ing-gê-ris?
broken	pecah	pê-chah
broken down (car, machine)	rosak	ro-sak

English	Malay	Pronunciation
brother (elder)	abang	ah-bang
(younger brother)	adik lelaki	ah-dik-lé-la-kee
brown	perang	pe-rang
brush	berus	bê-rus
bucket	baldi	bal-dee
bulb (light)	mentol	men-tol
burglary	rompakan	rom-pa-kan
there's been a burglary	ada rompakan	ah-da rom-pa-kan
burn	bakar	ba-kar
to burn	membakar	mêm-ba-kar
I've burned my hand	Saya terbakar tangan sendiri	Sa-ya têr-ba-kar ta-ngan sên-dee-ree
burnt	terbakar	têr-ba-kar
it's burnt	ia terbakar	ee-ya têr-ba-kar
bus	bas	bas
can I go by bus?	boleh saya pergi dengan bas?	bo-leh sa-ya pêr-gee dê-ngan bas?
the bus to the beach	bas menuju ke pantai	bas mê-noo-joo kê pan-tai
the bus to the shopping centre	bas menuju ke pusat membeli-belah	bas mê-noo-joo kê poo-sat mêm-bê-lee bê-lah
business	perniagaan	pêr-nia-ga-an
bus station	stesen bas	steh-sen bas
where is the bus station?	di manakah stesen bas?	dee ma-na-kah steh-sen bas?
bus stop	perhentian bas	pêr-hên-tee-yan bas
where is the bus stop?	di manakah perhentian bas?	dee ma-na-kah pêr-hên-tee-yan bas?
busy	sibuk	si-buk
I'm busy	Saya sibuk	Sa-ya si-buk
butcher's	kedai penjual daging	kê-dai pên-joo-wal da-ging
butter	mentega	mên-te-ga
to buy	membeli	mêm-bê-lee

can I buy this?	boleh saya beli ini?	bo-leh sa-ya bê-lee ee-nee?	**camera**	kamera	ka-me-ra
where can I buy bread?	di mana boleh saya beli roti?	dee-ma-na bo-leh sa-ya bê-lee ro-tee?	**to camp**	berkhemah	bêr-khe-mah
where can I buy milk?	di mana boleh saya beli susu?	dee-ma-na bo-leh sa-ya bê-lee soo-soo?	**camp site**	tapak perkhemahan	ta-pak pêr-khe-ma-han
by	dengan	dê-ngan	*no camping*	dilarang berkhemah	dee-la-rang bêr-khe-mah
by bus	dengan bas	dê-ngan bas	**can** (tin)	tin	tin
by train	dengan keretapi	dê-ngan kê-re-ta-pee	*a can of oil*	setin minyak	sê-tin mee-niak
			cancel	batal	ba-tal
C			*I want to cancel my booking*	Saya hendak membatalkan penempahan saya	Sa-ya hên-dak mêm-ba-tal-kan pê-nêm-pa-han sa-ya
café	kafe	ka-fe	**candle**	lilin	li-lin
cake	kek	kek	**can opener**	pembuka tin	pêm-boo-ka tin
cake shop	kedai kek	kê-dai kek	**car**	kereta	kê-re-ta
to call (on phone)	menelefon	mê-ne-le-fon	*by car*	dengan kereta	dê-ngan kê-re-ta
camcorder	kamera video	ka-me-ra vee-dee-yo	**car park**	tempat letak kereta	têm-pat lê-tak kê-reta
			car seat (for child)	kerusi kereta budak	kê-roo-see kê-re-ta boo-dak

English	Malay	Pronunciation
car wash	cuci kereta	choo-chi kê-re-ta
card	kad	kad
cards (playing)	terup	tê-rup
carpet (rug)	permaidani	pêr-mai-da-nee
carry	bawa	ba-wa
cash	tunai	too-nai
I have no cash	Saya tak ada wang tunai	Sa-ya tak ah-da wang too-nai
to cash	menunaikan	mê-noo-nai-kan
cash desk	meja tunai	me-ja too-nai
castle	istana	is-ta-nai
cat	kucing	koo-ching
caution	hati-hati	ha-tee-ha-tee
cave	gua	goo-wa
CD	CD	see-dee
do you have it on CD?	anda ada CDnya?	an-da ah-da see-dee-nia?
CD player	pemain CD	pê-main see-dee
cemetery	tanah perkuburan	ta-nah pêr-koo-bu-ran
central	pusat	poo-sat
central station	stesen utama	steh-sen oo-tama
town centre	pusat bandar	poo-sat ban-dar
certificate	sijil	see-jil
chain	rantai	ran-tai
chair	kerusi	kê-roo-see
champagne	arak champagne	ah-rak shem-pen
change (loose coins)	duit syiling	doo-wit shee-ling
keep the change	simpan bakinya	sim-pan ba-kee-nia
where's my change?	mana duit baki saya?	ma-na doo-wit ba-kee sa-ya?
to change (money)	menukar	mê-noo-kar
where can I change money?	di mana boleh saya tukar wang?	dee ma-na bo-leh sa-ya too-kar wang?
changing room (fee)	bilik salinan bayaran	ba-lik sa-li-nan ba-ya-ran
cheap	murah	moo-rah

English – Malay

English	Malay	Pronunciation
I want the cheapest	Saya hendak yang paling murah	Sa-ya hên-dak yang pa-ling moo-rah
check	periksa	pê-rik-sa
to check in	daftar masuk	daf-tar ma-suk
what time should I check in?	pada pukul berapa patut saya daftar masuk?	pa-da poo-kul bê-ra-pa pa-tut sa-ya daf-tar ma-suk?
cheers!	selamat!	sê-la-mat!
cheese	keju	ke-joo
chemist's	kedai farmasi	kê-dai far-ma-see
night duty chemist	ahli farmasi malam	ah-lee far-ma-see ma-lam
where is the chemist?	di mana ahli farmasi?	dee ma-na ah-lee far-ma-see?
cheque	cek	cek
cheque book	buku cek	boo-koo chek
Travellers Cheques	cek kembara	cek kêm-ba-ra
cherry	ceri	che-ree
chest (of body)	dada	da-da
chewing gum	gula-gula getah	goo-la goo-la gê-tah
chickenpox	cacar air	cha-cha ah-yer
child	kanak-kanak	ka-nak-ka-nak
chips	cip	chip
chocolate	cokelat	cho-kê-lat
hot chocolate	cokelat panas	cho-kê-lat pa-nas
chop (meat)	chop	chop
Christmas	Hari Krismas	Ha-ree Kris-mas
church	gereja	gê-re-ja
cigar	cerut	che-root
cigarettes	rokok	ro-kok
a packet of cigarettes	sekotak rokok	sê-ko-tak ro-kok
cinema	panggung wayang	pang-gung wa-yang

English	Malay	Pronunciation
what's on at the cinema?	apa yang sedang ditayangkan di panggung wayang?	ah-pa yang sê-dang dee-ta-yang-kan dee pang-gung wa-yang?
where is the cinema?	di manakah panggung wayang?	dee ma-na-kah pang-gung wa-yang?
city	bandar	ban-dar
city centre	pusat bandar	poo-sat ban-dar
clean	bersih	bêr-sih
it's not clean	ia tak bersih	ee-ya tak bêr-sih
to clean	membersihkan	mêm-bêr-sih-kan
please clean my room	tolong bersihkan bilik saya	toh-long bêr-sih-kan bee-lik sa-ya
please clean the bath	tolong bersihkan bilik air	toh-long bêr-sih-kan bee-lik ah-yer
climbing	mendaki	mên-da-kee
to go climbing	mendaki	mên-da-kee
clock	jam	jam
close	dekat	dê-kat
is it close by?	dekat tak?	dê-kat tak?
to close	menutup	mê-noo-tup
when does it close?	bilakah ia akan ditutup?	bee-la-kah ee-ya ah-kan dee-too-tup?
closed	sudah ditutup	soo-dah dee-too-tup
is it closed?	sudah ditutupkah?	soo-dah dee-too-tup kah?
clothes	pakaian	pa-ka-yan
coast	pantai	pan-tai
coat	kot	kot
cocoa	koko	ko-ko
cockroach	lipas	lee-pas
coconut	kelapa	kê-la-pa
coffee	kopi	ko-pee
black coffee	kopi o	ko-pee o
iced coffee	kopi ais	ko-pee ais
instant coffee	kopi segera	ko-pee sê-gê-ra
coin	syiling	shee-ling
Coke®	Coke®	Coke

English – Malay

English	Malay	Pronunciation	English	Malay	Pronunciation
cold	selsema	sêl-sê-ma	conditioner (for hair)	perapi	pê-ra-pee
I have a cold	Saya menghidap selsema	Sa-ya mêng-hee-dap sêl-sê-ma	condoms	kondom	kon-dom
to be cold	sejuk	sê-juk	conference	persidangan	pêr-see-da-ngan
I'm cold	Saya sejuk	Sa-ya sê-juk	to confirm	mengesahkan	mê-ngê-sah-kan
I'd like a cold drink	Saya mahu minuman sejuk	Sa-ya ma-hoo mi-noo-man sê-juk	congratulations!	tahniah!	tah-nee-yah!
colour	warna	war-na	connection (train, plane)	penyambung (keretapi, kapalterbang)	pê-niam-bung (kê-rê-ta-pee, ka-pal-têr-bang)
comb	sikat	see-kat	I missed my connection (bus, train, plane)	Saya ketinggalan penyambung (bas, keretapi, kapalterbang)	Sa-ya kê-teeng-ga-lan (bas, kê-re-ta-pee, ka-pal-têr-bang) pê-niam-bung
to come (arrive)	datang	da-tang			
come in!	masuk!	ma-suk!			
comfortable	selesa	sê-le-sa	consulate	konsulat	kon-soo-lat
company (business)	syarikat	sha-ree-kat	American Consulate	konsulat Amerika	kon-soo-lat Ah-me-ree-ka
compass	kompas	kom-pas	British Consulate	konsulat British	kon-soo-lat Bri-tish
complaint	aduan	ah-doo-wan	contact lens	kanta lekap	kan-ta lê-kap
computer	komputer	kom-poo-têr			
concert	konsert	kon-sêrt			
pop concert	konsert pop	kon-sêrt pop			

English	Malay	Pronunciation
I've lost my contact lenses	Saya kehilangan kanta lekap	Sa-ya kê-hee-la-ngan kan-ta lê-kap
contact lens cleaner	pencuci kanta lekap	pên-choo-chee kan-ta lê-kap
contraceptive pill	pil perancang	pil pê-ran-chang
to cook	memasak	mê-ma-sak
cooker	dapur masak	da-pur ma-sak
copy	salin	sa-lin
to copy (photocopy)	menyalin (fotokopi)	mê-nia-lin (fo-to-ko-pee)
corkscrew	pencabut gabus	pên-cha-but ga-bus
corner	sudut	soo-doot
cot	katil budak	ka-til boo-dak
cost	kos	kos
how much does it cost?	berapa kosnya?	bê-ra-pa kos-nia?
cotton (material)	kapas (kain)	ka-pas (ka-yin)
is it cotton?	kain kapas kah?	ka-yin ka-pas kah?
to cough	batuk	ba-tuk
counter (desk)	kaunter	kaun-têr
country (not town)	desa	de-sa
couple (two people)	pasangan	pa-sa-ngan
crash (collision)	berlanggar	bêr-lang-gar
crash helmet	topi keledar	to-pee kê-le-dar
cream (dairy)	krim (tenusu)	krim (tê-noo-soo)
credit card	kad kredit	kad kreh-deet
I've lost my credit card	Saya kehilangan kad kredit	Sa-ya kê-hee-la-ngan kad kreh-deet
to cry (weep)	menangis	mê-na-ngis
cucumber	timun	tee-mun
cup	cawan	cha-wan
cushion	kusyen	koo-shên
customs	kastam	kas-tam
customs control	kawalan kastam	ka-wa-lan kas-tam

English – Malay

cut	potong	po-tong
to cut	memotong	mê-mo-tong
to cycle (bicycle)	mengayuh	mê-nga-yuh
bicycle	basikal	ba-see-kal

D

daily	harian	ha-ree-yan
damage	kerosakan	kê-ro-sa-kan
dance	tarian	ta-ree-yan
to dance	menari	mê-na-ree
danger	bahaya	ba-ha-ya
dangerous	berbahaya	bêr-ba-ha-ya
dark	gelap	gê-lap
date (calendar)	tarikh (kalendar)	ta-rikh (ka-len-dar)
date of birth	tarikh lahir	ta-rikh la-hir
daughter	anak perempuan	ah-nak pê-rem-poo-wan
what is the date?	apa tarikh hari ini?	ah-pa ta-rikh ha-ree-ee-nee?
day	hari	ha-ree

every day	setiap hari	sê-ti-yap ha-ree
deaf	pekak	pê-kak
decaffeinated coffee	kopi nyahkafeina	ko-pee nyah-ka-fey-na
December	Disember	Dee-sem-bêr
deck chair	kerusi malas	kê-roo-see ma-las
deep	dalam	da-lam
delay	penangguhan	pê-nang-gu-han
is there a delay?	ada penangguhan kah?	ah-da pê-nang-gu-han kah?
delicatessen	makanan istimewa	ma-ka-nan is-tee-me-wa
delicious	enak	eh-nak
this is delicious!	enaknya!	eh-nak-nia!
dentist	doktor gigi	dok-tor gee-gee
dentures	gigi palsu	gee-gee pal-soo
deodorant	deodoran	deo-do-ran
department store	gedung serba ada	gê-dung sêr-ba ah-da
departures	berlepas	bêr-lê-pas

English	Malay	Pronunciation
deposit	deposit	dee-po-sit
dessert	pencuci mulut	pĕn-choo-chee moo-lut
detergent	detergen	dee-tĕr-gen
diabetic	penghidap kencing manis	pĕng-hee-dap kĕn-ching ma-nis
dialling code	kod pendailan	kod pĕn-dai-lan
diamond	permata	pĕr-ma-ta
diarrhoea	cirit-birit	che-ret be-ret
diary	diari	dee-ya-ree
dictionary	kamus	ka-mus
diesel	disel	dee-sel
where can I get diesel?	di mana boleh saya dapatkan disel?	dee ma-na bo-leh sa-ya da-pat-kan dee-sel?
diet	diet	da-yĕt
I'm on a diet	Saya sedang berdiet	Sa-ya sĕ-dang bĕr-da-yĕt
different	lain	la-yin
difficult	susah	soo-sah
it's difficult	ia susah	ee-ya soo-sah
dinghy	selekeh	sĕ-le-keh
dining room	ruang makan	roo-ang ma-kan
dinner (evening meal)	makan malam	ma-kan ma-lam
direct	terus	tê-roos
is it a direct train?	ini keretapi terus kah?	ee-nee kê-re-ta-pee tê-roos kah?
direct flight	penerbangan terus	pê-nêr-ba-ngan tê-roos
directory (telephone)	direktori (telefon)	de-rek-to-ree (te-le-fon)
dirty	kotor	ko-tor
disabled (person)	kurang upaya	koo-rang oo-pa-ya
disco	disko	dis-ko
discount	diskaun	dis-kaun
disease	penyakit	pê-nia-kit
disinfectant	pembasmi kuman	pêm-bas-mee koo-man
distilled water	air suling	ah-yer soo-ling
to dive	menyelam	mê-nyê-lam

English – Malay

English	Malay	Pronunciation
divorced	bercerai	bêr-chê-rai
I'm divorced	Saya sudah bercerai	Sa-ya soo-dah bêr-chê-rai
dizzy	pening	pê-ning
I feel dizzy	Saya rasa pening	Sa-ya ra-sa pê-ning
doctor	doktor	dok-tor
documents	dokumen	do-koo-mên
where are the documents?	di manakah dokumen-dokumen itu?	dee ma-na-kah do-koo-mên-do-koo-mên ee-too?
dog	anjing	an-jing
doll	patung	pa-tung
door	pintu	peen-too
double bed	katil kelamin	ka-til kê-la-min
double room	bilik kelamin	bee-lik kê-la-min
downstairs	di tingkat bawah	dee ting-kat ba-wah
dozen	dozen	do-zen
drain	longkang	long-kang
drawer	laci	la-chee
dress	gaun	gaun
drink	minuman	mee-noo-man
to drink	minum	mee-noom
drinking water	air minuman	ah-yer mee-noo-man
to drive	memandu	mê-man-doo
driver	pemandu	pê-man-doo
driving licence	lesen memandu	le-sen mê-man-doo
to drown	lemas	lê-mas
drug (medicinal)	dadah, ubat	da-dah, oo-bat
drunk	mabuk	ma-buk
I'm drunk	Saya mabuk	Sa-ya ma-buk
dry	kering	kê-ring
dry cleaner's	pencuci kering	pên-choo-chee kê-ring
dust	habuk	ha-buk
duty free	bebas cukai	be-bas choo-kai

E

English	Malay	Pronunciation
ear	telinga	tê-lee-nga

English	Malay		English	Malay	
earache	sakit telinga	sa-kit-tê-lee-nga	empty	kosong	ko-song
I have earache	Saya sakit telinga	Sa-ya sa-kit tê-lee-nga	end	tamat	ta-mat
early	awal	ah-wal	engaged (to be married)	bertunang	bêr-too-nang
earrings	anting-anting	an-ting-an-ting	it's engaged (phone, toilet)	sedang digunakan	sê-dang dee-goo-na-kan
earthquake	gempa bumi	gêm-pa boo-mee	engine	enjin	en-jin
east	timur	tee-mur	England	England	Ing-glên
easy	mudah	moo-dah	English	Inggeris	Ing-gê-ris
to eat	memakan	mê-ma-kan	do you speak English?	anda boleh bertutur dalam bahasa Inggeris?	an-da bo-leh bêr-too-tur da-lam ba-ha-sa Ing-gê-ris?
egg	telur	tê-lur			
elastic band	gelang elastik	gê-lang ee-las-tik	I'm English	Saya orang Inggeris	Sa-ya oh-rang Ing-gê-ris
electric	elektrik	ee-lek-trik	enjoy	suka	soo-ka
electric razor	pisau cukur elektrik	pee-sau choo-kur ee-lek-trik	I enjoy swimming	Saya suka berenang	Sa-ya soo-ka bê-rê-nang
e-mail	e-mel	ee-mel	I enjoy playing tennis	Saya suka main tenis	Sa-ya soo-ka ma-yin te-nis
embassy	kedutaan	kê-doo-ta-an			
American Embassy	Kedutaan Amerika	Kê-doo-ta-an Ah-me-ree-ka	enough	cukup	choo-kup
British Embassy	Kedutaan British	Kê-doo-ta-an Bri-tish			
emergency	kecemasan	kê-chê-ma-san			

English – Malay

English – Malay

English	Malay	Pronunciation
it's not enough	ia tak cukup	ee-ya tak choo-kup
enquiry desk	meja	me-ja
pertanyaan	pêr-ta-nia-an	
to enter	memasuki	mê-ma-su-kee
entertainment	hiburan	hee-boo-ran
entrance	pintu masuk	pin-too ma-suk
where is the	di manakah	dee ma-na-kah
entrance?	pintu masuk?	pin-too ma-suk?
entrance fee	yuran masuk	yoo-ran ma-suk
envelope	sampul	sam-pul
escape	melarikan diri	mê-la-ree-kan dee-ree
fire escape	tangga	tang-ga
kecemasan	kê-chê-ma-san	
Europe	Eropah	Eh-ro-pah
evening	petang	pê-tang
evening meal	makanan	ma-ka-nan
petang	pê-tang	

English	Malay	Pronunciation
this evening	petang ini	pê-tang ee-nee
tomorrow	petang esok	pê-tang êh-sok
evening	setiap	sê-tee-yap
every	setiap hari	sê-tee-yap ha-ree
every year	setiap tahun	sê-tee-yap ta-hun
everyone	setiap orang	sê-tee-yap oh-rang
excellent	cemerlang	chê-mêr-lang
exchange	tukar	too-kar
exchange rate	kadar	ka-dar
pertukaran	pêr-too-ka-ran	
exciting	menyeronokkan	mê-nyê-ro-nok-kan
excuse me!	maafkan saya!	ma-af-kan sa-ya!
exhibition	pameran	pa-me-ran
exit	pintu keluar	pin-too kê-loo-war
emergency exit	pintu keluar	pin-too kê-loo-war kê-chê-ma-san
kecemasan	kê-chê-ma-san	

English	Malay	Pronunciation
where is the exit?	di manakah pintu keluar?	dee ma-na-kah pin-too kê-loo-war?
expensive	mahal	ma-hal
to expire	luput	loo-poot
to explain	menerangkan	mê-nê-rang-kan
please explain	sila terangkan	see-la tê-rang-kan
extra	tambahan	tam-ba-han
eye	mata	ma-ta
F		
face	muka	moo-ka
factory	kilang	kee-lang
to faint	pengsan	peng-san
to fall	jatuh	ja-tuh
family	keluarga	kê-loo-war-ga
my family	keluarga saya	kê-loo-war-ga saya
famous	terkenal	têr-kê-nal
fan	kipas	kee-pas
far	jauh	ja-wuh
is it far?	jauhkah?	ja-wuh-kah?
fare (train, bus, etc.)	tambang	tam-bang
how much is the fare?	berapakah tambangnya?	bê-ra-pa-kah tam-bang-nia?
farm	ladang	la-dang
farmer	peladang	pê-la-dang
fashion	fesyen	fe-shên
fast	cepat	chê-pat
fat	gemuk	gê-muk
father	bapa	ba-pa
my father	bapa saya	ba-pa-sa-ya
father-in-law	bapa mertua	ba-pa mêr-too-wa
my father-in-law	bapa mertua saya	ba-pa mêr-too-wa sa-ya
fault (defect)		
favourite	kegemaran	kê-gê-ma-ran
February	Febuari	Fe-boo-wa-ree
feel	rasa	ra-sa
I don't feel well	Saya rasa tidak sihat	Sa-ya ra-sa tee-dak see-hat

English – Malay

English	Malay	Pronunciation
I feel sick	Saya rasa loya	Sa-ya ra-sa-lo-ya
I feel tired	Saya rasa penat	Sa-ya ra-sa pê-nat
ferry	feri	fe-ree
few	sedikit	sê-dee-kit
fiancé(e)	tunang	too-nang
to fill (up)	mengisi	mê-ngee-see
fill it up!	isi sampai penuh!	ee-see sam-pai pê-nuh!
film	filem	fee-lêm
filter	tapis	ta-pis
to find	mencari	mên-cha-ree
I can't find my passport	Saya tak jumpa pasport saya	Sa-ya tak joom-pa pas-port sa-ya
I can't find my wallet	Saya tak jumpa dompet saya	Sa-ya tak joom-pa dom-pet sa-ya
fine (to be paid)	denda	dên-da
fine (weather)	baik	ba-yik
finish	tamat	ta-mat
when does it finish?	bilakah ia akan tamat?	bee-la-kah ee-ya ah-kan ta-mat?
fire	api	ah-pee
fire alarm	penggera api	pêng-gê-ra ah-pee
fire brigade	bomba	bom-ba
fire exit	pintu	peen-too
fire extinguisher	kecemasan pemadam api	kê-chê-ma-san pê-ma-dam ah-pee
fireworks	bunga api	boo-nga ah-pee
first	pertama	pêr-ta-ma
the first bus	bas pertama	bas pêr-ta-ma
the first train	keretapi pertama	kê-re-ta-pee pêr-ta-ma
first aid	bantuan kecemasan	ban-too-wan kê-chê-ma-san
first class	kelas pertama	kê-las pêr-ta-ma
first floor	tingkat pertama	ting-kat pêr-ta-ma
fish	ikan	ee-kan
to fish	memancing	mê-man-ching
fisherman	nelayan	nê-la-yan
fit	padan	pa-dan

English	Malay	
it doesn't fit me	ia tak padan dengan saya	ee-ya tak pa-dan dê-ngan sa-ya
fix	baiki	bai-kee
can you fix it?	boleh anda baiki?	bo-leh an-da bai-kee?
flash (for camera)	denyar	dê-niar
flat (apartment)	flat (apartmen)	flat (apart-men)
flat	rata	ra-ta
flavour	perisa	pê-ree-sa
flight	penerbangan	pê-nêr-ba-ngan
flood	banjir	ban-jir
floor	lantai	lan-tai
flour	tepung	tê-pung
flower	bunga	boo-nga
flu	demam selsema	dê-mam sêl-sê-ma
fly	terbang	têr-bang
to fly	terbang	têr-bang
fog	kabus	ka-bus
folder	folder	fol-dêr
to follow	mengekori	mê-nge-ko-ree
that man is following me	lelaki itu mengekori saya	lê-la-kee ee-too mê-nge-ko-ree sa-ya
food	makanan	ma-ka-nan
foot	kaki	ka-kee
football (game)	bola sepak	bo-la se-pak
for	untuk	oon-tuk
for me	untuk saya	oon-tuk sa-ya
for sale	untuk dijual	oon-tuk
forbidden	dilarang	dee-joo-wal
forecast (weather)	ramalan	ra-ma-lan
foreign	asing	ah-sing
forest	hutan	hoo-tan
forever	selama-lamanya	sê-la-ma-la-ma-nia
to forget	terlupa	têr-loo-pa

English – Malay

English	Malay	Pronunciation
I've forgotten my key	Saya terlupa kunci saya	Sa-ya ter-loo-pa koon-chee sa-ya
fork (for eating)	garpu	gar-poo
forward(s)	ke depan	kê dê-pan
free (unoccupied)	kosong	ko-song
(costing nothing)	percuma	pêr-choo-ma
freezer	peti ais	pê-tee ais
French	Perancis	Pê-ran-chis
frequent	kerap	kê-rap
fresh	segar	sê-gar
fresh fish	ikan segar	ee-kan sê-gar
fresh fruit	buah-buahan segar	boo-wah boo-wah-an sê-gar
fresh milk	susu segar	soo-soo sê-gar
fresh vegetables	sayur-sayuran segar	sa-yur-sa-yur-an sê-gar
is it fresh?	ia segar kah?	ee-ya sê-gar kah?
Friday	Jumaat	Joo-ma-at
fridge	peti sejuk	pê-tee sê-juk
fried (food)	goreng	go-reng

English	Malay	Pronunciation
friend	kawan	ka-wan
from	daripada	da-ree-pa-da
front	depan	dê-pan
can I sit in the front?	boleh saya duduk di depan?	bo-leh sa-ya doo-duk dee dê-pan?
front door	pintu depan	peen-too dê-pan
frozen	beku	bê-koo
fruit	buah	boo-wah
fruit juice	jus buah	jus boo-wah
fruit salad	salad buah	sa-lad boo-wah
fuel	bahan api	ba-han ah-pee
full	penuh	pê-nuh
furniture	perabot	pê-ra-bot

G

English	Malay	Pronunciation
gallery (art)	galeri (lukisan)	ga-le-ree (loo-kee-san)
game (sport)	permainan (sukan)	pêr-ma-yi-nan (soo-kan)
garden	halaman	ha-la-man

see GRAMMAR

English	Malay	Pronunciation
garlic	bawang putih	ba-wang poo-tih
gas	gas	gas
gate	get	get
genuine	sebenar	sê-bê-nar
German	orang Jerman	oh-rang jêr-man
Germany	Jerman	jêr-man
to get	mendapat	mên-da-pat
to get into	memasuki	mê-ma-soo-kee
to get on board	menaiki	mê-nai-kee
to get off (bus, etc.)	turun	too-run
gift	hadiah	ha-dee-yah
gift shop	kedai hadiah	kê-dai ha-dee-yah
girl	budak perempuan	boo-dak pê-rêm-poo-wan
girlfriend	teman wanita	tê-man wa-nee-ta
to give (give back)	memberi (memulangkan)	mêm-bê-ree (mê-moo-lang-kan)
give way	memberi laluan	mêm-bê-ree la-loo-wan

English	Malay	Pronunciation
glass (for drink)	gelas	gê-las
a glass of water	segelas air	sê-gê-las ah-yer
a glass of wine	segelas wain	sê-gê-las wain
to go	pergi	pêr-gee
to go back	pulang	poo-lang
to go in	masuk	ma-suk
to go out	keluar	kê-loo-war
gold	emas	ê-mas
golf	golf	golf
golf ball	bola golf	bo-la golf
golf club	kayu golf	ka-yoo golf
good	baik	ba-yik
goodbye	selamat jalan	sê-la-mat ja-lan
good day	selamat siang	sê-la-mat see-yang
goodnight	selamat malam	sê-la-mat ma-lam
grandfather	datuk	da-tuk
grandmother	nenek	ne-nek
grapes	anggur	ang-goor
greasy	berminyak	bêr-mee-niak

English – Malay

it's too greasy (food)	ia terlalu berminyak	ee-ya têr-la-loo bêr-mee-niak		
green	hijau	hee-jau	hair	rambut	ram-but
greengrocer's	kedai penjual sayur	kê-dai pên-joo-wal sa-yur	hair dryer	pengering rambut	pê-ngê-ring ram-but
grey	kelabu	kê-la-boo	hair-brush	berus rambut	bê-rus ram-but
grilled	bakar	ba-kar	haircut	gunting rambut	goon-ting ram-but
grocer's	kedai runcit	kê-dai roon-chit	hairdresser	pendandan	pên-dan-dan
group (of people)	kumpulan	kum-poo-lan		rambut	ram-but
			half	setengah	sê-tê-ngah
guarantee	jamin	ja-min	*half bottle*	setengah botol	sê-tê-ngah bo-tol
guest	tetamu	tê-ta-moo	*half an hour*	setengah jam	sê-tê-ngah jam
guesthouse	rumah	roo-mah	ham	daging babi	da-ging ba-bee
			hand	tangan	ta-ngan
guide/ guidebook	panduan/buku panduan	toom-pa-ngan pan-doo-wan/ boo-koo pan-doo-wan	hand luggage	bagasi tangan	ba-ga-see ta-ngan
			handbag	beg tangan	beg ta-ngan
			handmade	buatan tangan	boo-wa-tan ta-ngan
guided tour	lawatan berpandu	la-wa-tan bêr-pan-doo			
			to happen	jadi	ja-dee
			what happened?	apa telah terjadi?	ah-pa tê-lah têr-ja-dee?

English – Malay

happy	gembira	gêm-bee-ra	herbs	herba	hêr-ba
hard (tough)	liat	lee-yat	here	di sini	dee see-nee
hat	topi	to-pee	high	tinggi	ting-gee
he	dia	dee-ya	high blood pressure	tekanan darah tinggi	tê-ka-nan da-rah ting-gee
head	kepala	kê-pa-la	high chair	kerusi tinggi budak	kê-roo-see ting-gee boo-dak
headache	sakit kepala	sa-kit kê-pa-la	to hire (rent)	mengupah, menyewa	mê-ngoo-pah, mê-nyeh-wa
I've got a headache	Saya sakit kepala	Sa-ya sa-kit kê-pa-la	*I want to hire a car*	Saya mahu menyewa kereta	Sa-ya ma-hoo mê-nyeh-wa kê-re-ta
to hear	mendengar	mên-dê-ngar	to hitchhike	mengembara tumpang	mê-ngêm-ba-ra toom-pang
heart	jantung	jan-tung	holiday	cuti	choo-tee
heart attack	serangan jantung	sê-ra-ngan jan-tung	home	kediaman	kê-dee-ya-man
heating	memanas	mê-ma-nas	honey	madu	ma-doo
heavy	berat	bê-rat	honeymoon	bulan madu	boo-lan ma-doo
height	ketinggian	kê-ting-gee-yan	*we're on honeymoon*	kami sedang berbulan madu	ka-mee sê-dang bêr-boo-lan ma-doo
hello	helo	he-lo			
help!	tolong!	toh-long!			
to help	menolong, membantu	mê-no-long, mêm-ban-too			
can you help me?	boleh anda bantu saya?	bo-leh an-da ban-too sa-ya?			

English – Malay

horse	kuda	koo-da
hospital	hospital	hos-pee-tal
to the hospital, please	tolong pergi ke hospital	toh-long pêr-gee kê hos-pee-tal
hot	panas	pa-nas
it's too hot	ia terlalu panas	ee-ya têr-la-loo pa-nas
hotel	hotel	ho-tel
hour	jam	jam
in an hour's time	dalam masa sejam	da-lam ma-sa sê-jam
house	rumah	roo-mah
how?	bagaimana?	ba-gai-ma-na?
how are you?	apa khabar?	ah-pa kha-bar?
how many?	berapa?	bê-ra-pa?
how much?	berapa banyak?	bê-ra-pa ba-niak?
hungry	lapar	la-par
I'm hungry	Saya lapar	Sa-ya la-par
hurry	cepat	chê-pat
I'm in a hurry	Saya nak cepat	Sa-ya nak chê-pat
hurt	sakit	sa-kit

it hurts	ia menyakitkan	ee-ya mê-nia-kit-kan
husband	suami	soo-wa-mee
my husband	suami saya	soo-wa-mee sa-ya
I	Saya	Sa-ya
ice	ais	ais
ice cream	ais krim	ais krim
iced coffee	kopi o ais	ko-pee o ais
iced tea	teh o ais	teh o ais
iced water	ais kosong	ais ko-song
identification card	kad pengenalan	kad pê-ngê-na-lan
ill	uzur	oo-zur
I'm ill	Saya uzur	Sa-ya oo-zur
immediately	serta-merta	sêr-ta mêr-ta
important	mustahak	moos-ta-hak
impossible	tidak mungkin	tee-dak mung-kin
it's impossible	ia tidak mungkin	ee-ya tee-dak mung-kin

English	Malay	Pronunciation
included	termasuk	têr-ma-suk
is insurance	termasuk	têr-ma-suk
included?	insuran?	in-soo-ran?
indigestion	tidak hadam	tee-dak ha-dam
infection	jangkitan	jang-ki-tan
information	maklumat	mak-loo-mat
information office	pejabat maklumat	pê-ja-bat mak-loo-mat
injured	tercedera	têr-chê-dê-ra
I've been injured	Saya tercedera	Sa-ya
insect	serangga	sê-rang-ga
insect bite	gigitan serangga	gee-gee-tan sê-rang-ga
insect repellent	pengusir serangga	pê-ngoo-sir sê-rang-ga
instant coffee	kopi segera	ko-pee sê-gê-ra
insurance	insuran	in-soo-ran
interesting	menarik	mê-na-rik
international	antarabangsa	an-ta-ra-bang-sa
interpreter	penterjemah	pên-têr-jê-mah

English	Malay	Pronunciation
to invite	mengundang	mê-ngoon-dang
invoice	invois	in-vois
Ireland	Ireland	Air-lên
Irish	orang Ireland	oh-rang Air-lên
iron (metal)	besi	bê-see
iron (for clothes)	seterika	sê-tê-ree-ka
island	pulau	poo-lau
it	ia	ee-ya
Italian	orang Itali	oh-rang Ee-ta-lee
Italy	Itali	Ee-ta-lee
itch	gatal	ga-tal

J

English	Malay	Pronunciation
jacket	jaket	ja-ket
leather jacket	jaket kulit	ja-ket koo-lit
jam (food)	jem	jem
January	Januari	Ja-noo-wa-ree
jar	balang	ba-lang
jeans	seluar jean	sê-loo-war jeen
jellyfish	ubur-ubur	oo-bur-oo-bur

English	Malay	Pronunciation
jewellery	barang kemas	ba-rang kê-mas
Jewish	Yahudi	Ya-hoo-dee
I'm Jewish	Saya orang Yahudi	Sa-ya oh-rang Ya-hoo-dee
job	pekerjaan	pê-kêr-ja-an
what's your job?	apa pekerjaan anda?	ah-pa pê-kêr-ja-an an-da?
joke	jenaka	jê-na-ka
it's a joke	itu gurau senda	ee-too gurau sên-da
journalist	wartawan	war-ta-wan
journey	perjalanan	pêr-ja-la-nan
juice	jus	jus
orange juice	jus oren	jus oh-ren
tomato juice	jus tomato	jus to-ma-to
July	Julai	Joo-lai
June	Jun	Jun
K		
to keep	menyimpan	mê-nyim-pan
	simpan bakinya	sim-pan ba-kee-nia
keep the change		
key	kunci	koon-chee
my key, please	tolong berikan saya kunci	toh-long bê-ree-kan sa-ya koon-chee
kind	baik	ba-yik
you're very kind	anda sangat baik	an-da sa-ngat men-chee-yoom
to kiss	mencium	mên-chee-yoom
kitchen	dapur	da-pur
knee	lutut	loo-tut
knife	pisau	pee-sau
to know	mengetahui	mê-ngê-ta-hoo-wee
I know	Saya tahu	Sa-ya ta-hoo
I don't know	Saya tak tahu	Sa-ya tak ta-hoo
L		
ladies' (toilet)	tandas wanita	tan-das wa-nee-ta
larger	lebih besar	lê-bih bê-sar

English	Malay	Pronunciation
lake	tasik	ta-sik
lamp	lampu	lam-poo
land	mendarat	mên-da-rat
has the plane landed?	kapalterbang sudah mendarat?	ka-pal-têr-bang soo-dah / mên-da-rat?
landing	sedang mendarat	sê-dang / mên-da-rat
late	lambat	lam-bat
sorry I'm late	maaf, saya lambat	ma-af, sa-ya / lam-bat
later	nanti	nan-tee
laundry service	khidmat dobi	khid-mat doh-bee
lawyer	peguam	pê-goo-wam
leather	kulit	koo-lit
to leave	pergi	pêr-gee
we leave tomorrow	kami akan berangkat esok	ka-mee ah-kan / bêr-ang-kat eh-sok
left	kiri	kee-ree

English	Malay	Pronunciation
left-luggage office	pejabat simpan bagasi	pê-ja-bat sim-pan / ba-ga-see
leg	kaki	ka-kee
lemonade	air lemonad	ah-yer le-mo-nad
to lend	meminjamkan	mê-min-jam-kan
to let (allow)	membenarkan	mêm-bê-nar-kan
licence (driving)	lesen	le-sen
lifeboat	bot penyelamat	bot pê-nyê-la-mat
lifeguard	penyelamat	pê-nye-la-mat
	lemas	lê-mas
life jacket	jaket keselamatan	ja-ket / kê-sê-la-ma-tan
lift (elevator)	lif	lif
light (illumination)	lampu	lam-poo
do you have a light?	anda ada pemetik api?	an-da ah-da pê-mê-tik ah-pee?
light bulb	mentol lampu	men-tol lam-poo
lighter (cigarette)	pemetik api	pê-mê-tik ah-pee

English	Malay	Pronunciation	English	Malay	Pronunciation
to like	suka	soo-ka	long	lama	la-ma
I like coffee	Saya suka kopi	Sa-ya soo-ka ko-pee	how long will it take?	Berapa lama?	Bê-ra-pa la-ma?
I don't like coffee	Saya tak suka kopi	Sa-ya tak soo-ka ko-pee	to look after someone	menjaga	mên-ja-ga
linen	linen	lee-nên	to look for	mencari	mên-cha-ree
lipstick	gincu	gin-choo	lost	hilang	hee-lang
to listen to	mendengar	mên-dê-ngar	lot	lot	lot
to litter (rubbish)	membuang sampah	mêm-boo-wang sam-pah	a lot	banyak	ba-niak
little (small)	kecil	kê-chil	lotion	losyen	lo-shên
just a little, please	tolong berikan saya sedikit sahaja	toh-long bê-ree-kan sa-ya sê-dee-kit sa-ha-ja	loud	kuat	koo-wat
to live	menetap	mê-nê-tap	to love (romantic love)	menyintai, menyayangi	mê-nyin-ta-ee, mê-nia-ya-ngee
I live in London	Saya menetap di London	Sa-ya mê-nê-tap dee London	I love you	Aku cinta pada mu	Ah-koo chin-ta pa-da moo
lock	kunci	koon-chee	lovely	cantik	chan-tik
to lock	mengunci	mê-ngoon-chee	lucky	bertuah	bêr-too-wah
locker (for luggage)	loker	lo-kêr	luggage	bagasi	ba-ga-see
			lunch	makan tengahari	ma-kan tê-nga-ha-ree

M

English	Malay	Pronunciation
maid	pembantu rumah	pêm-ban-too roo-mah
main course (of meal)	hidangan utama	hee-da-ngan oo-ta-ma
to make	membuat	mêm-boo-wat
man	lelaki	lê-la-kee
manager	pengurus	pê-ngoo-rus
map	peta	pê-ta
March	Mac	Mach
married	berkahwin	bêr-kah-win
are you married?	anda sudah berkahwin?	an-da soo-dah bêr-kah-win?
I'm married	Saya sudah berkahwin	Sa-ya soo-dah bêr-kah-win
I'm not married	Saya bujang	Sa-ya boo-jang
match (game)	perlawanan	pêr-la-wa-nan
matches (light)	mancis	man-chis
maximum speed	kelajuan maksimum	kê-la-joo-wan mak-see-moom
May	Mei	Mey

English	Malay	Pronunciation
meal	makanan	ma-ka-nan
mean	maksud	mak-sud
what does it mean?	apa maksudnya?	ah-pa mak-sud-nia?
measure	ukur	oo-kur
can I measure it?	boleh saya ukurkannya?	bo-leh sa-ya oo-kur-kan-nia?
meat	daging	da-ging
medicine	ubat	oo-bat
to meet	berjumpa	bêr-joom-pa
meeting	mesyuarat	mê-shoo-wa-rat
menu	menu	me-noo
the menu, please	tolong bawa menu	toh-long ba-wa me-noo
message	pesanan	pê-sa-nan
are there any messages?	ada apa-apa pesanan?	ah-da ah-pa-ah-pa pê-sa-nan?
meter (taxi)	meter (teksi)	mee-têr (tek-see)
microwave (oven)	ketuhar gelombang mikro	kê-too-har gê-lom-bang mee-kro

English – Malay

midday	tengahari	tê-nga-ha-ree	
middle	tengah	tê-ngah	
midnight	tengah malam	tê-ngah ma-lam	
milk	susu	soo-soo	
mineral water	air mineral	ah-yer mee-nê-ral	
mints	gula-gula pudina	goo-la goo-la poo-dee-na	
minute	minit	mee-neet	
mirror	cermin	chêr-min	
miss (plane, train, etc.)	ketinggalan	kê-teeng-ga-lan	
I missed the bus	Saya ketinggalan bas	Sa-ya kê-teeng-ga-lan bas	
missing (thing)	hilang	hee-lang	
my wallet is missing	dompet saya hilang	dom-pet sa-ya hee-lang	
mistake	silap	see-lap	
Monday	Isnin	Is-nin	
money	duit	doo-wit	
month	bulan	boo-lan	
moon	bulan	boo-lan	

more	lagi	la-gee	
some more...	lagi...	la-gee...	
more bread, please	tolong berikan saya roti lagi	toh-long bê-ree-kan sa-ya ro-tee la-gee	
morning	pagi	pa-gee	
in the morning	pada waktu	pa-da wak-too pa-gee	
this morning	pagi ini	pa-gee ee-nee	
tomorrow morning	pagi esok	pa-gee eh-sok	
mosque	masjid	mas-jid	
mosquito net	kelambu	kê-lam-boo	
mosquitoes	nyamuk	nia-muk	
mother	ibu	ee-boo	
mother-in-law	ibu mertua	ee-boo mêr-too-wa	
motorway	lebuh raya	lê-buh ra-ya	
mountain	gunung	goo-nung	
mouse	tikus	tee-kus	
moustache	misai	mee-sai	

English	Malay	Pronunciation
mouth	mulut	moo-lut
much	banyak	ba-niak
how much?	berapa banyak?	bê-ra-pa ba-niak?
it's too much	ini terlalu	ee-nee têr-la-loo
too much (too expensive)	mahal	ma-hal
too much	banyak sangat	ba-niak sa-ngat
museum	muzium	moo-zee-yoom
music shop	kedai muzik	kê-dai moo-zik
Muslim	Muslim	Mus-lim
mustard	mustard	mas-tad

N

nail (metal)	paku	pa-koo
nail polish	cat kuku	chat koo-koo
nail polish remover	pembersih cat kuku	pêm-bêr-sih chat koo-koo
name	nama	na-ma
my name is	nama saya	na-ma sa-ya
what's your name?	apa nama anda?	ah-pa na-ma an-da?

English	Malay	Pronunciation
napkin	kertas kesat tangan	kêr-tas kê-sat ta-ngan
narrow	sempit	sêm-pit
nationality	kewarganegaraan	kê-war-ga-nê-ga-ra-an
navy blue	biru laut	bee-roo la-wut
near	dekat	dê-kat
is it near?	dekat kah?	dê-kat kah?
necessary	perlu	pêr-loo
is it necessary to book?	perlu tempah kah?	pêr-loo têm-pah kah?
neck	leher	le-her
to need	perlu, memerlukan	pêr-loo, mê-mêr-loo-kan
I need	Saya perlu	Sa-ya pêr-loo
I need a car	Saya perlu sebuah kereta	Sa-ya pêr-loo sê-boo-wah kê-re-ta
I need to go	Saya perlu berangkat	Sa-ya pêr-loo bêr-ang-kat
needle	jarum	ja-rum

English – Malay

English	Malay	Pronunciation
a needle and thread	jarum dan benang	ja-rum dan bê-nang
neighbour	jiran	jee-ran
nephew	anak saudara lelaki	ah-nak sau-da-ra lê-la-kee
new	baru	ba-roo
never	tidak pernah	tee-dak pêr-nah
news	berita	bê-ree-ta
newspaper	suratkhabar	soo-rat-kha-bar
an English newspaper	suratkhabar Inggeris	soo-rat-kha-bar Ing-gê-ris
New Year	Tahun Baru	Ta-hun Ba-roo
New Zealand	New Zealand	New Zee-lên
when is the next boat?	bilakah bot yang seterusnya?	sê-tê-roos-nia? yang sê-tê-roos-nia?
when is the next bus?	bilakah bas yang seterusnya?	bee-la-kah bas yang sê-tê-roos-nia?
next to	di sebelah	dee-sê-bê-lah
nice	bagus	ba-gus
it's very nice	bagus betul	ba-gus bê-tul
we had a nice time	kami terhibur	ka-mee têr-hee-boor
niece	anak saudara perempuan	ah-nak sau-da-ra pê-rêm-poo-wan
night	malam	ma-lam
last night	semalam	sê-ma-lam
nightclub	kelab malam	kê-lab ma-lam
no	tidak	tee-dak
no, thanks	tak apa, terima kasih	tak ah-pa, tê-ree-ma ka-sih
noisy	bising	bee-sing
non-alcoholic	tanpa alkohol	tan-pa al-ko-hol
a non-alcoholic drink	minuman tanpa alkohol	mee-noo-man tan-pa al-ko-hol
none	tak ada	tak ah-da
there's none left	sudah habis	soo-dah ha-bis
non-smoking	dilarang merokok	dee-la-rang mê-ro-kok

English	Malay	Pronunciation
north	utara	oo-ta-ra
Northern Ireland	Ireland Utara	Air-liên Oo-ta-ra
nose	hidung	hee-dung
not	tidak	tee-dak
notebook	buku nota	boo-koo no-ta
nothing	tak ada apa-apa	tak ah-da ah-pa ah-pa
November	November	No-vem-bêr
now	sekarang	sê-ka-rang
number	nombor	nom-bor
phone number	nombor telefon	nom-bor-te-le-fon
number plate	plet nombor	plet nom-bor
nurse	jururawat	joo-roo-ra-wat
nuts (bar nibbles)	kacang	ka-chang

O

English	Malay	Pronunciation
October	Oktober	Ok-to-bêr
octopus	sotong	so-tong
off (radio, engine, etc.)	padam	pa-dam
this is off (milk, food)	ini sudah basi	ee-nee soo-dah ba-see
office	pejabat	pê-ja-bat
I work in an office	Saya kerja di sebuah pejabat	Sa-ya kêr-ja dee sê-boo-wah pê-ja-bat
often	kerap	kê-rap
oil	minyak	mee-niak
OK	OK	oh-kay
old (age)	umur/usia	oo-mur/oo-see-ya
(years)	tahun	ta-hun
(elderly)	tua	too-wa
how old are you?	berapa umur anda?	bê-ra-pa oo-mur an-da?
how old is it? (building, etc.)	berapa usianya?	bê-ra-pa oo-see-ya-nia?
I'm ... years old...	Saya berumur ...tahun	Sa-ya bêr-oo-mur ... ta-hun
olives	zaitun	zai-toon

English – Malay

English	Malay	Pronunciation
olive oil	minyak zaitun	mee-niak zai-toon
on	hidup	hee-dup
see GRAMMAR		
once	sekali	sê-ka-lee
at once	sekarang juga	sê-ka-rang joo-ga
one	satu	sa-too
onion	bawang	ba-wang
only	hanya	ha-nia
only one	hanya satu	ha-nia sa-too
open	buka	boo-ka
is it open?	ia sudah dibuka?	ee-ya soo-dah dee-boo-ka?
to open	membuka	mêm-boo-ka
opening hours	waktu buka	wak-too boo-ka
operator (telephone)	operator	oh-pe-ra-tor
opposite	bertentangan dengan	bêr-tên-ta-ngan dê-ngan
optician	pakar optik	pa-kar op-tik
or	atau	ah-tau
orange (colour)	jingga	jing-ga
orange	buah oren	boo-wah oh-ren
orange juice	jus oren	jus oh-ren
to order (food)	memesan	mê-mê-san
other	lain	la-yin
our	kami	ka-mee
out	keluar	kê-loo-war
he's gone out	dia sudah keluar	dee-ya soo-dah kê-loo-war
out	rosak	ro-sak
out of order	rosak	ro-sak
oven	ketuhar	kê-too-har
to overtake	memotong	mê-mo-tong
to owe	hutang	hoo-tang
what do I owe you?	berapa perlu saya bayar?	bê-ra-pa pêr-loo sa-ya-bayar?
you owe me ...	anda perlu bayar saya ...	an-da pêr-loo ba-yar sa-ya ...
owner	tuan punya	too-wan poo-nia

P

English	Malay	Pronunciation
to pack (bags)	mengemas	mê-ngê-mas

English		Malay	
package tour	pakej pelancongan	meletak kereta	mê-lê-tak kê-re-ta
packet	bungkus	rakan niaga	ra-kan nee-ya-ga
paid	sudah bayar	pasangan saya	pa-sa-ngan sa-ya
I've already paid	Saya sudah bayar		
painful	menyakitkan	majlis	maj-lis
it's very painful	ia sangat menyakitkan	penumpang	pê-noom-pang
painkiller	ubat tahan sakit	passport	pas-port
painting (picture)	lukisan	pasta	pas-ta
pair	pasang	bayar	ba-yar
palace	istana	di mana patut saya bayar?	dee ma-na pa-tut sa-ya ba-yar?
pancake	penkek	kacang tanah	ka-chang ta-nah
pants (trousers)	seluar	mutiara	moo-tee-ya-ra
		pejalan kaki	pê-ja-lan ka-kee
paper	kertas	lintasan pejalan kaki	leen-ta-san pê-ja-lan ka-kee
pardon!	maaf!	pen	pen
parents	ibu bapa	pensel	pen-sel
park	taman	penisilin	pe-nee-see-leen

to park	meletak kereta
partner (business)	rakan niaga
my partner (in couple)	pasangan saya
party (celebration)	majlis
passenger	penumpang
passport	passport
pasta	pasta
to pay	bayar
where do I pay?	di mana patut saya bayar?
peanuts	kacang tanah
pearl	mutiara
pedestrian	pejalan kaki
pedestrian crossing	lintasan pejalan kaki
pen	pen
pencil	pensel
penicillin	penisilin

English – Malay

English	Malay	Pronunciation
pepper (spice)	lada hitam	la-da hee-tam
per	setiap	sê-tee-yap
per hour	setiap jam	sê-tee-yap jam
per kilometre	setiap kilometer	sê-tee-yap kee-lo-mee-têr
per week	setiap minggu	sê-tee-yap ming-goo
perfect	sempurna	sêm-pur-na
it's perfect	ia sempurna	ee-ya-sêm-pur-na
performance	persembahan	pêr-sêm-ba-han
perfume	minyak wangi	mee-niak wa-ngee
permit	permit	per-mit
do I need a permit?	saya perlu permit kah?	sa-ya pêr-loo pêr-mit kah?
person	orang	oh-rang
per person	setiap orang	sê-tee-yap oh-rang
petrol	petrol	pe-trol
unleaded petrol	petrol tanpa plumbum	pe-trol tan-pa ploom-boom
petrol station	stesen petrol	steh-sen pe-trol
phone	telefon	te-le-fon
phonecard	kad telefon	kad te-le-fon
photocopy	fotokopi	fo-to-ko-pee
photograph	fotograf	fo-to-graf
picnic	berkelah	bêr-ke-lah
picture (on wall)	gambar	gam-bar
pie	pai	pai
piece (slice)	keping	kê-ping
pill	pil	pil
pillow	bantal	ban-tal
pin	pin	pin
pink	merah jambu	me-rah jam-boo
pipe (for smoking)	paip	pa-yip
pipe (drain, etc.)	saluran	sa-lu-ran
plain	biasa	bee-ya-sa
plane	kapalterbang	ka-pal-têr-bang
plastic	plastik	plas-tik
plate	pinggan	ping-gan
platform	platform	plat-form

English	Malay	pronunciation
(railway) *platform?*	platform yang mana?	plat-form yang ma-na?
which platform?		
to play	main	ma-yin
please	tolong	toh-long
plug (electric)	palam	pa-lam
plumber	tukang paip	too-kang pa-yip
pocket	kocek	ko-chek
poisonous	beracun	bĕ-ra-chun
police	polis	po-lis
police station	stesen polis	steh-sen po-lis
polish (for shoes)	pengilat	pĕ-ngee-lat
pool	kolam	ko-lam
is there a pool?	ada tak kolam?	ah-da tak ko-lam?
poor (not rich)	miskin	mis-kin
pork	daging babi	da-ging ba-bee
port (harbour)	pelabuhan	pĕ-la-bu-han
possible	mungkin	mung-kin
to post	mengepos	mĕ-ngĕ-pos
postbox	peti surat	pĕ-tee soo-rat

English	Malay	pronunciation
postcard	poskad	pos-kad
postcode	poskod	pos-kod
poster	poster	pos-ter
post office	pejabat pos	pĕ-ja-bat pos
where is the post office?	di manakah pejabat pos?	dee ma-na-kah pĕ-ja-bat pos?
pot (for cooking)	periuk	pĕ-ree-yuk
potato	ubi kentang	oo-bee kĕn-tang
boiled potatoes	ubi kentang rebus	oo-bee kĕn-tang rĕ-bus
fried potatoes	ubi kentang goreng	oo-bee kĕn-tang go-reng
mashed potato	ubi kentang lenyek	oo-bee kĕn-tang leh-nyek
potato salad	salad kentang	sa-lad kĕn-tang
powdered milk	susu tepung	soo-soo tĕ-pung
prawns	udang	oo-dang
to prefer	lebih suka	lĕ-bih soo-ka
I'd prefer tea	Saya lebih suka teh	Sa-ya lĕ-bih soo-ka teh

English – Malay

English	Malay	Pronunciation
pregnant	hamil	ha-mil
I'm pregnant	Saya hamil	Sa-ya ha-mil
prescription	preskripsi	pres-kree-see
present (gift)	hadiah	ha-dee-yah
this is a present	ini hadiah	ee-nee ha-dee-yah
pretty	cantik	chan-tik
price	harga	har-ga
price list	senarai harga	sē-na-rai har-ga
private	persendirian	pēr-sēn-dee-ree-yan
private bathroom	bilik air persendirian	bee-lik ah-yer pēr-sēn-dee-ree-yan
probably	barangkali	ba-rang-ka-lee
to pronounce	menyebut	mē-nyē-but
how is this pronounced?	bagaimana hendak menyebut ini?	ba-gai-ma-na hēn-dak mē-nyē-but ee-nee?
public holiday	cuti umum	choo-tee oo-mum
pudding	puding	poo-ding
to pull	menarik	mē-na-rik
purple	ungu	oo-ngoo
to push	menolak	mē-no-lak
pushchair	kereta sorong	kē-re-ta so-rong
pyjamas	baju tidur	ba-joo tee-dur
Q		
quality	kualiti	koo-wa-lee-tee
good quality	kualiti bagus	koo-wa-lee-tee ba-gus
poor quality	kualiti buruk	koo-wa-lee-tee boo-ruk
queen	permaisuri	pēr-mai-soo-ree
question	soalan	so-ah-lan
queue	barisan	ba-ri-san
to queue	berbaris	bēr-ba-ris
quickly	cepat-cepat	chē-pat chē-pat
quiet	senyap	sē-niap
quilt	kulit	koo-wit

R

English	Malay	Pronunciation			
rabbit	arnab	ar-nab			
rabies	penyakit anjing gila	pê-nia-kit an-jing gee-la			
race (sport)	lumba (sukan)	loom-ba (soo-kan)			
radio	radio	ra-di-yo			
radish	lobak	lo-bak			
rain	hujan	hoo-jan			
raincoat	baju hujan	ba-joo hoo-jan			
raisins	kismis	kis-mis			
rare (steak)	kurang masak	koo-rang ma-sak			
rash (skin)	ruam	roo-wam			
rat	tikus	tee-kus			
rate	kadar	ka-dar			
exchange rate	pertukaran	pêr-too-ka-ran			
raw ham	daging babi mentah	da-ging ba-bee mên-tah			
razor	pisau cukur	pee-sau choo-kur			
to read (book)	membaca	mêm-ba-cha			
ready	siap	see-yap			

English	Malay	Pronunciation
is it ready?	sudah siap?	soo-dah see-yap?
real	betul	bê-tul
is it real gold?	ini emas betul?	ee-nee ê-mas bê-tul?
is it real leather?	ini kulit betul?	ee-nee koo-lit bê-tul?
receipt	resit	reh-sit
reception (desk)	tempat	têm-pat
to recommend	menyambut	mê-nyam-but
	tetamu	tê-ta-moo
recipe	resipi	re-see-pee
red	saran	sa-ran
red wine	merah	me-rah
reduction	wain merah	wain me-rah
to refund	diskaun	dis-kaun
I'd like a refund	bayar balik	ba-yar ba-lik
	Saya mahu	Sa-ya ma-hoo
	bayaran balik	ba-ya-ran ba-lik
regulations	peraturan	pêr-ah-too-ran
relation (family member)	saudara	sau-da-ra

English – Malay

English	Malay	Pronunciation
reliable (person, service)	boleh diharap	bo-leh dee-ha-rap
to remember	ingat	ee-ngat
rent	sewa	seh-wa
how much is the rent?	berapa sewanya?	bê-ra-pa seh-wa-nia?
to rent	menyewa	mê-nyeh-wa
to repair	membaiki	mêm-bai-kee
to repeat	mengulang	mê-ngoo-lang
reservation	penempahan	pê-nêm-pa-han
to reserve (room, table, etc.)	menempah	mê-nêm-pah
reserved	ditempah	dee-têm-pah
to rest	berehat	bê-re-hat
I need to rest	Saya perlu berehat	Sa-ya pêr-loo bê-re-hat
restaurant	restoran	res-toh-ran
retired	bersara	bêr-sa-ra
to return	kembali	kêm-ba-lee
return (ticket)	dua hala	doo-wa ha-la
reverse-charge call	panggilan pindah bayaran	pang-gee-lan pin-dah ba-ya-ran
rice (cooked)	nasi	na-see
rich (person)	kaya	ka-ya
right (correct)	betul	bê-tul
on/to the right	di sebelah kanan	dee sê-bê-lah ka-nan
ring (for finger)	cincin	chin-chin
river	sungai	soo-ngai
road	jalan	ja-lan
is this the road to ...?	inikah jalan yang menuju ke ...?	ee-nee-kah ja-lan yang mê-noo-joo kê ...?
road map	peta jalan	pê-ta ja-lan
roof	atap	ah-tap
room	bilik	bee-lik
room service	khidmat bilik	khid-mat bee-lik
rope	tali	ta-lee
rose	mawar	ma-war
rotten (food)	basi	ba-see

route	jalan	ja-lan
what's the best route?	apakah jalan terbaik?	ah-pa-kah ja-lan tĕr-ba-yik?
rubber	getah	gĕ-tah
rug	permaidani	pĕr-mai-da-nee

S

sad	sedih	sĕ-dih
safe	peti besi	pĕ-tee bĕ-see
safe	selamat	sĕ-la-mat
is it safe to swim?	adakah selamat untuk berenang?	ah-da-kah sĕ-la-mat oon-tuk bĕ-rĕ-nang?
safety pin	pin dawai	pin da-wai
sailing	berlayar	bĕr-la-yar
sale	jualan	joo-wa-lan
for sale	untuk dijual	oon-tuk dee-joo-wal
salad	salad	sa-lad
salesperson	jurujual	joo-roo-joo-wal
salmon	salmon	sal-mĕn

salt	garam	ga-ram
same	sama	sa-ma
sand	pasir	pa-sir
sandals	sandal	san-dal
sardines	sardin	sar-din
Saturday	Sabtu	Sab-too
sauce	sos	sos
sausage	sosej	so-sej
to say	berkata	bĕr-ka-ta
please say that again	tolong katakan lagi	toh-long ka-ta-kan la-gee
what did you say?	apa anda kata?	ah-pa an-da ka-ta?
school	sekolah	sĕ-ko-lah
scissors	gunting	goon-ting
Scotland	Scotland	Skot-lĕn
Scottish	orang Scotland	oh-rang Skot-lĕn
I'm Scottish	Saya orang Scotland	Sa-ya oh-rang Skot-lĕn
sculpture	ukiran	oo-kee-ran
sea	laut	la-wut

English – Malay

seafood	makanan laut	ma-ka-nan la-wut	
seasick	mabuk laut	ma-buk la-wut	
I'm feeling seasick	Saya rasa mabuk laut	Sa-ya ra-sa ma-buk la-wut	
seat (chair)	kerusi	kê-roo-see	
reserved seat	kerusi khas	kê-roo-see khas	
seat belt	tali pinggang	ta-lee ping-gang	
	keledar	kê-le-dar	
second	kedua	kê-doo-wa	
second class	kelas kedua	kê-las kê-doo-wa	
a second class ticket	tiket kê-las	tee-ket kê-las kê-doo-wa	
secondhand	terpakai	têr-pa-kai	
to see	tengok	te-ngok	
to sell	menjual	mên-joo-wal	
to send	menghantar	mêng-han-tar	
senior citizen	warga tua	war-ga too-wa	
separate	asing	ah-sing	
separately	berasingan	bêr-ah-sing-an	
September	September	Sep-tem-bêr	
serious	serius	see-ree-yus	
is it serious?	seriuskah?	see-ree-yus-kah?	
service	khidmat	khid-mat	
service charge	caj perkhidmatan	chaj pêr-khid-ma-tan	
shade (shadow)	bayang-bayang	ba-yang-ba-yang	
shampoo	syampu	sham-poo	
to shave	mencukur	mên-choo-kur	
shaver	pencukur	pên-choo-kur	
shaving cream	krim pencukuran	krim pên-choo-ku-ran	
she	dia	dee-ya	
sheet (for bed)	cadar	cha-dar	
shelf	para	pa-ra	
shell	cengkerang	chêng-kê-rang	
shellfish	kerang-kerangan	kê-rang kê-ra-ngan	
I don't eat shellfish	Saya tak makan kerang-kerangan	Sa-ya tak ma-kan kê-rang kê-ra-ngan	
ship	kapal	ka-pal	
shirt	kemeja	kê-me-ja	

shoes	kasut	ka-sut	signature	tandatangan	tan-da-ta-ngan
shop	kedai	kê-dai	silk	sutera	soo-tê-ra
shop assistant	pembantu kedai	pêm-ban-too kê-dai	is it silk?	ini sutera kah?	ee-nee soo-tê-ra kah?
shopping	membeli-belah	mêm-bê-lee bê-lah	silver	perak	peh-rak
short	pendek	pen-dek	is it silver?	ini perak kah?	ee-nee peh-rak kah?
shorts (short trousers)	seluar pendek	sê-loo-war pen-dek	simple	mudah	moo-dah
show	tunjuk	tun-juk	single (one)	satu	sa-too
to show	menunjuk	mê-nun-juk	single (unmarried)	bujang	boo-jang
shower (bath)	bilik mandi	bee-lik man-dee	I'm single	Saya bujang	Sa-ya boo-jang
	dengan	dé-ngan	single room	bilik bujang	bilik boo-jang
	pancuran	pan-choo-ran	sink	sinki	sing-kee
shrimps	udang	oo-dang	sister (elder)	kakak	ka-kak
shut	tutup	too-tup	sister (younger)	adik	ah-dik
to shut	menutup	mê-noo-tup	sit	duduk	doo-duk
sick	loya	lo-ya	size (shoes)	saiz	saiz
I feel sick	Saya rasa loya	Sa-ya ra-sa lo-ya	bigger size	saiz lebih besar	saiz lê-bih bê-sar
sign (road, notice)	tanda	tan-da	smaller size	saiz lebih kecil	saiz lê-bih kê-chil
to sign (form, cheque, etc.)	menandatangani	mê-nan-da-ta-nga-nee			

English – Malay

to skate	menggeluncur	mêng-gê-loon-choor
skates	penggeluncur	pêng-gê-loon-choor
skimmed milk	susu skim	soo-soo skim
skin	kulit	koo-lit
skirt	skirt	skirt
sky	langit	la-ngit
to sleep	tidur	tee-dur
sleeping bag	beg tidur	beg tee-dur
sleeping pill	pil tidur	pil tee-dur
slice	hiris	hee-ris
slippers	selipar	sê-lee-par
slow	perlahan	pêr-la-han
small	kecil	kê-chil
smaller	lebih kecil	lê-bih kê-chil
smell	bau	ba-woo
to smell	membau	mêm-ba-woo
smile	senyum	sê-nyum
smoke	asap	ah-sap
to smoke	merokok	mê-ro-kok

I don't smoke	Saya tak merokok	Sa-ya tak mê-ro-kok
please don't smoke	tolong jangan merokok	toh-long ja-ngan mê-ro-kok
snake	ular	oo-lar
soap	sabun	sa-bun
socks	stokin	sto-kin
soft	lembut	lêm-but
soft drink	minuman	mee-noo-man
	bergas	bêr-gas
sold out	habis dijual	ha-bis dee-joo-wal
some	sesetengah	sê-sê-tê-ngah
someone	seseorang	sê-sê-oh-rang
something	sesuatu	sê-soo-wa-too
sometimes	kadang-kadang	ka-dang-ka-dang
son	anak lelaki	ah-nak lê-la-kee
song	lagu	la-goo
soon	tak lama lagi	tak la-ma la-gee
sorry	maaf	ma-af
I'm sorry!	Minta maaf!	Meen-ta ma-af!

English	Malay	Pronunciation
sort (type)	isih (jenis)	ee-sih (jě-nis)
soup	sup	soop
south	selatan	sě-la-tan
souvenir	cenderamata	chěn-dě-ra-ma-ta
souvenir shop	kedai cenderamata	kě-dai chěn-dě-ra-ma-ta
to speak	bertutur	běr-too-toor
do you speak English?	anda boleh bertutur dalam bahasa Inggeris?	an-da bo-leh běr-too-toor da-lam ba-ha-sa Ing-gě-ris?
I don't speak Malay	Saya tak boleh bertutur dalam bahasa Melayu	Sa-ya tak bo-leh běr-too-toor da-lam ba-ha-sa Mě-la-yoo
special	istimewa	is-tee-me-wa
speed	kelajuan	kě-la-joo-wan
spell	eja	eh-ja
how do you spell it?	bagaimana hendak mengejanya?	ba-gai-ma-na hěn-dak měng-eh-ja-nia?
spicy	pedas	pě-das
sponge (for cleaning)	span	sparn
spoon	sudu	soo-doo
sport	sukan	soo-kan
squid	sotong	so-tong
stadium	stadium	sta-dee-yoom
stairs	tangga	tang-ga
stamp	setem	stem
star	bintang	bin-tang
to start	memulakan	mě-moo-la-kan
when does it start?	bilakah ia akan bermula?	bee-la-kah ee-ya ah-kan běr-moo-la?
station	stesen	steh-sen
bus station	stesen bas	steh-sen bas
railway station	stesen keretapi	steh-sen kě-re-ta-pee
to stay	menginap	mě-ngee-nap
I'm staying at the ... Hotel	Saya menginap di Hotel ...	Sa-ya mě-ngee-nap dee Ho-tel...

English – Malay

English	Malay	Pronunciation
steep	curam	choo-ram
is it steep?	curam kah?	choo-ram kah?
still (not fizzy)	tanpa karbonat	tan-pa kar-bo-nat
stomach	perut	pê-rut
stop!	berhenti!	bêr-hên-tee!
storm	ribut	ree-but
straight on	jalan terus	ja-lan tê-roos
keep straight on	jalan terus	ja-lan tê-roos
straw	stro	stro
(for drinking)		
street	jalan	ja-lan
street map	peta jalan	pê-ta ja-lan
string	tali	ta-lee
strong (tea, coffee)	pekat	pê-kat
stuck	melekat	mê-lê-kat
it's stuck	ia melekat	ee-ya mê-lê-kat
student	penuntut	pê-noon-tut
stung	disengat	dee-sê-ngat
I've been stung	Saya telah disengat	Sa-ya tê-lah dee-sê-ngat
stupid	bodoh	bo-doh
sugar	gula	goo-la
suit (clothes)	sut	soot
suitcase	beg pakaian	beg pa-ka-yan
I've lost my suitcase	Saya kehilangan beg pakaian	Sa-ya kê-hee-la-ngan beg pa-ka-yan
summer	musim panas	moo-sim pa-nas
in summer	dalam musim panas	da-lam moo-sim pa-nas
sun	matahari	ma-ta-ha-ree
sunbathe	berjemur	bêr-jê-moor
sunburn	terkena selaran matahari	têr-kê-na sê-la-ran ma-ta-ha-ree
Sunday	Ahad	Ah-had
sunglasses	cermin mata gelap	chêr-min ma-ta gê-lap
sunshade	payung	pa-yung
suntan lotion	losyen pelindung matahari	lo-shên pê-leen-dung ma-ta-ha-ree

supermarket	pasar raya	pa-sar-ra-ya
supplement	tambahan	tam-ba-han
surfboard	papan luncur	pa-pan loon-choor
surfing	meluncur	mê-loon-choor
surname	nama bapa	na-ma ba-pa
sweater	baju sejuk	ba-joo sê-juk
sweet	manis	ma-nis
sweetener	pemanis	pê-ma-nis
sweets	gula-gula	goo-la goo-la
to swim	berenang	bê-rê-nang
swimming pool	kolam renang	ko-lam rê-nang
is there a swimming pool?	ada tak kolam renang?	ah-da tak ko-lam rê-nang?
swimsuit	baju mandi	ba-joo man-dee
switch	suis	soo-wis
to switch off	memadamkan	mê-ma-dam-kan
to switch on	menghidupkan	mêng-hee-doop-kan

| swollen (finger, ankle, etc.) | bengkak | bêng-kak |

T

table	meja	me-ja
table tennis	ping pong	ping pong
to take	mengambil	mê-ngam-bil
can I take pictures?	boleh saya ambil gambar?	bo-leh sa-ya am-bil gam-bar?
will you take a picture of us?	boleh anda ambil gambar kami?	bo-leh an-da am-bil gam-bar ka-mee?
to talk	bercakap	bêr-cha-kap
tall	tinggi	ting-gee
tap (knock)	ketuk	kê-tuk
tap (water tap)	paip	paip
tape (cassette)	pita	pee-ta
taste	rasa	ra-sa
can I taste some?	boleh saya rasa sedikit?	bo-leh sa-ya ra-sa sê-dee-kit?
tasty	sedap	sê-dap

English – Malay

English	Malay	Pronunciation
tax	cukai	choo-kai
taxi	teksi	tek-see
tea	teh	teh
teacher	guru	goo-roo
team (football, etc.)	pasukan	pa-soo-kan
teeth	gigi	gee-gee
telephone	telefon	te-le-fon
to telephone	menelefon	mê-ne-le-fon
can I telephone	boleh saya	bo-leh sa-ya
	menelefon	mê-ne-le-fon
from here?	dari sini?	da-ree see-nee?
telephone box	pondok telefon	pon-dok te-le-fon
telephone call	panggilan	pang-gee-lan
	telefon	te-le-fon
international	panggilan	pang-gee-lan an-
call	antarabangsa	ta-ra-bang-sa
telephone	direktori telefon	di-rek-to-ree
directory		te-le-fon
television	televisyen	te-le-vee-shên
temperature	demam, suhu	dê-mam,
(fever)		soo-hoo
I have a	Saya demam	Sa-ya dê-mam
temperature		
what is the	berapa	bê-ra-pa
temperature?	suhunya?	soo-hoo-nia?
temporary	sementara	sê-mên-ta-ra
tennis	tenis	te-nis
do you play	anda boleh	an-da bo-leh
tennis?	main tenis?	ma-yin te-nis?
I'd like to play	Saya suka	Sa-ya soo-ka
tennis	main tenis	ma-yin te-nis
tennis ball	bola tenis	bo-la te-nis
tennis court	gelanggang	gê-lang-gang
	tenis	te-nis
tennis racket	raket tenis	ra-ket tê-nis
tent	khemah	khe-mah
terrace	teres	teh-res
tetanus	tetanus	teh-ta-nus
thank you/	terima kasih	tê-ree-ma ka-sih
thanks		

English	Malay	
that	itu	ee-too
theatre	panggung	pang-goong
there	ada...	ah-da...
there is.../ there are	ada...	ah-da...
is there...?	ada tak...?	ah-da tak...?
these	ini	ee-nee
they	mereka	mê-re-ka
thief	pencuri	pên-choo-ree
thin	kurus	koo-roos
to think	memikir	mê-mee-kir
I think so	Saya fikir begitu	Sa-ya fee-kir bê-gee-too
I don't think so	Saya tidak fikir begitu	Sa-ya tee-dak fikir bê-gee-too
thirsty	haus	ha-wus
I'm thirsty	Saya haus	Sa-ya ha-wus
this	ini	ee-nee
those	itu	ee-too
thread	benang	bê-nang
Thursday	Khamis	Kha-mis
ticket	tiket	tee-ket
single ticket	tiket sehala	tee-ket sê-ha-la
return ticket	tiket dua hala	tee-ket doo-wa ha-la
ticket office	pejabat tiket	pê-ja-bat tee-ket
tie	tali leher	ta-lee le-her
tight	ketat	kê-tat
it's too tight	ia terlalu ketat	ee-ya têr-la-loo kê-tat
time	waktu	wak-too
timetable	jadual waktu	ja-doo-wal wak-too
tip (to waiter, etc.)	duit tip	doo-wit tip
tired	penat	pê-nat
tissues	tisu	tee-soo
to	ke	kê
see GRAMMAR		
to the station	ke stesen	kê steh-sen
toast	roti bakar	ro-tee ba-kar
today	hari ini	ha-ree ee-nee
together	bersama-sama	bêr-sa-ma sa-ma

English – Malay

English	Malay	Pronunciation
toilet	tandas	tan-das
toilet paper	tisu tandas	tee-soo tan-das
there is no toilet paper	tidak ada tisu tandas	tee-dak ah-da tee-soo tan-das
toll (on motorway, etc.)	tol	tol
tomato	tomato	to-ma-to
tomato juice	jus tomato	jus to-ma-to
tomato salad	salad tomato	sa-lad to-ma-to
tomorrow	esok	eh-sok
tomorrow evening	petang esok	pê-tang eh-sok
tomorrow morning	pagi esok	pa-gee eh-sok
tonight	malam ini	ma-lam ee-nee
tooth	gigi	gee-gee
toothache	sakit gigi	sa-kit gee-gee
toothbrush	berus gigi	bê-rus gee-gee
toothpaste	ubat gigi	oo-bat gee-gee
total	jumlah	joom-lah
tough (meat)	liat	lee-yat
tour	lawatan	la-wa-tan
tourist	pelancong	pê-lan-chong
tourist office	pejabat pelancong	pê-ja-bat pê-lan-chong
towel (hand towel)	tuala	too-wa-la
towel	tuala	too-wa-la
town	bandar	ban-dar
town hall	majlis bandaran	maj-lis ban-da-ran
toy	mainan	ma-yi-nan
traditional	tradisional	tra-dee-see-yo-nal
traffic	trafik	tra-fik
traffic lights	lampu trafik	lam-poo tra-fik
train	keretapi	kê-re-ta-pee
to translate	menterjemah	mên-têr-jê-mah
to travel	melancong	mê-lan-chong
travel agent	ejen pelancongan	eh-jen pê-lan-cho-ngan

English	Malay	Pronunciation
Travellers Cheques	cek kembara	chek kêm-ba-ra
tree	pokok	po-kok
trip	kunjungan	koon-joo-ngan
a day trip	kunjungan sehari	koon-joo-ngan sê-ha-ree
trousers	seluar	sê-loo-war
truck	trak	trak
true	benar	bê-nar
that's true	itu benar	ee-too bê-nar
that's not true	itu tidak benar	ee-too tee-dak bê-nar
try on	cuba	choo-ba
can I try it on?	boleh saya cuba?	bo-leh sa-ya choo-ba?
T-shirt	baju t	ba-joo tee
Tuesday	Selasa	Sê-la-sa
tuna	tuna	too-na
tunnel	terowong	tê-ro-wong
to turn off (radio, light)	memadamkan	mê-ma-damkan
to turn on	menghidupkan	mêng-hee-doop-kan
tweezers	pencabut	pên-cha-but
twins	kembar	kêm-bar

U

English	Malay	Pronunciation
ugly	hodoh	ho-doh
umbrella	payung	pa-yung
uncle	pakcik	pak-chik
uncomfortable	tak selesa	tak sê-le-sa
understand	faham	fa-ham
do you understand?	anda faham?	an-da fa-ham?
I don't understand	Saya tak faham	Sa-ya tak fa-ham
underwear	pakaian dalam	pa-ka-yan da-lam
unemployed	menganggur	me-ngang-gur
unleaded petrol	petrol tanpa plumbum	pe-trol tan-pa ploom-boom
university	universiti	oo-nee-vêr-see-tee

English – Malay

English	Malay	Pronunciation
unlucky	tak bernasib baik	tak bêr-na-sib ba-yik
upstairs	di tingkat atas	dee-ting-kat-ah-tas
urgent	penting	pên-ting
it's urgent	ia penting	ee-ya pên-ting
to use	menggunakan	mêng-goo-na-kan
useful	berguna	bêr-goo-na
usually	selalunya	sê-la-loo-nia
V		
vacancy (room)	kosong (bilik)	ko-song (bee-lik)
vacuum cleaner	pencuci hampagas	pên-choo-chee ham-pa-gas
valid	sah	sah
valuable	berharga	bêr-har-ga
van	van	van
VAT	cukai (tax)	choo-kai
veal	daging rusa	da-ging roo-sa
vegetable	sayur	sa-yur
vegetarian	vegetarian	ve-jee-ta-ri-yan
very	sangat	sa-ngat
very good	sangat baik	sa-ngat ba-yik
view	pemandangan	pê-man-da-ngan
village	kampung	kam-pung
visa	visa	vee-sa
to visit	melawat	mê-la-wat
visitor	pelawat	pê-la-wat
vitamin pills	pil vitamin	pil vee-ta-min
volleyball	bola lisut	bo-la lee-sut
W		
to wait (for)	menunggu	mê-noong-goo
please wait	sila tunggu	see-la toong-goo
waiter/waitress	pelayan	pê-la-yan
waiting room	bilik menunggu	bee-lik mê-noong-goo
to wake up	terjaga	têr-ja-ga
walk	jalan	ja-lan
to walk	berjalan	bêr-ja-lan
walking stick	tongkat	tong-kat
wallet	dompet	dom-pet

English	Malay	Pronunciation
to want	menghendaki	mêng-hên-da-kee
war	perang	pê-rang
wardrobe	almari	al-ma-ree
warm	hangat	ha-ngat
to wash	membasuh	mêm-ba-suh
washbasin	sinki	sing-kee
washing machine	mesin basuh	me-sin ba-suh
washing powder	serbuk pencuci	sêr-buk pên-choo-chee
wasp	penyengat	pê-nyê-ngat
watch (wrist)	jam tangan	jam ta-ngan
water	air	ah-yer
distilled water	air suling	ah-yer soo-ling
fresh water	air tawar	ah-yer ta-war
mineral water	air mineral	ah-yer mee-nê-ral
waterfall	air terjun	ah-yer têr-joon
waterproof	kalis air	ka-lis ah-yer
water-skiing	luncur air	loon-choor ah-yer
wave (sea)	ombak	om-bak
(hand)	lambai	lam-bai
way (method)	cara	cha-ra
(direction)	jalan	ja-lan
is this the right way?	ini jalan yang betul?	ee-nee ja-lan yang bê-tul?
way out	jalan keluar	ja-lan kê-loo-war
we	kami	ka-mee
	see GRAMMAR	
weak (tea, coffee, drink)	cair	cha-yer
to wear	memakai	mê-ma-kai
weather forecast	ramalan cuaca	ra-ma-lan choo-wa-cha
wedding	perkahwinan	pêr-kah-wi-nan
wedding ring	cincin perkahwinan	chin-chin pêr-kah-wi-nan
Wednesday	Rabu	Ra-boo
week	minggu	ming-goo
last week	minggu lepas	ming-goo lê-pas
next week	minggu depan	ming-goo dê-pan
weekend	hari minggu	ha-ree ming-goo

English – Malay

weekly	setiap minggu	sê-tee-yap ming-goo
weight	berat	bê-rat
welcome!	selamat datang	sê-la-mat da-tang
well	bagus	ba-gus
well done (meat)	cukup masak	choo-kup ma-sak
west	barat	ba-rat
wet	basah	ba-sah
what	apa	ah-pa
what is it?	apa dia?	ah-pa dee-ya?
wheelchair	kerusi roda	kê-roo-see ro-da
when?	bila?	bee-la?
where?	di mana?	dee ma-na?
which?	yang mana?	yang ma-na?
which one?	yang mana satu?	yang ma-na sa-too?
white	putih	poo-tih
who	siapa	see-ya-pa
whole	seluruh	sê-loo-ruh

whose	kepunyaan siapa	kê-poo-nia-an see-ya-pa
whose is it?	ini kepunyaan siapa?	ee-nee kê-poo-nia-an see-ya-pa?
why	kenapa/ mengapa	kê-na-pa/ mê-nga-pa
wife	isteri	is-tê-ree
window	tingkap	ting-kap
windy	berangin	bêr-ah-ngin
it's windy	beranginnya	bêr-ah-ngin-nia
wine	wain	wain
red wine	wain merah	wain me-rah
white wine	wain putih	wain poo-tih
wine list	senarai wain	sê-na-rai wain
with	dengan	dê-ngan
without	tanpa	tan-pa
woman	wanita	wa-nee-ta
wood (substance)	kayu	ka-yoo

see GRAMMAR

word	perkataan	pêr-ka-ta-an	
to work	berfungsi	bêr-foong-see	
it doesn't work	ia tidak berfungsi	ee-ya tee-dak bêr-foong-see	
wrap	balut	ba-lut	
please wrap it up	tolong balutkannia	toh-long ba-lut-kan-nia	
to write	menulis	mê-noo-lis	
writing paper	kertas tulisan	kêr-tas too-li-san	
wrong	salah	sa-lah	

X

X-ray	x-ray	x-ray	

Y

yacht	kapal pesiar	ka-pal pê-see-yar	
year	tahun	ta-hun	
this year	tahun ini	ta-hun ee-nee	
yellow	kuning	koo-ning	
yes	ya	ya	
yesterday	semalam	sê-ma-lam	

you	anda	an-da	

Z

zero	kosong	ko-song	
zip code	poskod	pos-kod	
zoo	zoo	zoo	

A

abang	elder brother
ada	there
ada...	there is...?
ada tak...?	there are
adik lelaki	is there...?
adik	younger brother
perempuan	younger sister
aduan	complaint
Ahad	Sunday
air	water
air lemonad	lemonade
air mineral	mineral water
air minuman	drinking water
air suling	distilled water
air tawar	fresh water
air terjun	waterfall
ais	ice
ais kosong	iced water
ais krim	ice cream

alah kepada	to be allergic to
alamat	address
alkohol	alcohol
almari	wardrobe
ambulan	ambulance
Amerika	America
anak lelaki	son
anak perempuan	daughter
anak saudara lelaki	nephew
anak saudara perempuan	niece
anda	you
anda ada mancis?	have you any matches?
anda ada risalah dalam bahasa Inggeris?	have you got a brochure in English?

anda terima Visa®?	do you accept Visa®?
anggur	grapes
anjing	dog
antarabangsa	international
anting-anting	earrings
apa	what
apa ada untuk sarapan pagi?	what is there for breakfast?
apa dia?	what is it?
apa khabar?	how are you?
apa patut saya bawa?	what should I bring?
apa saja	any
apa yang sedang ditayangkan di panggung wayang?	what's on at the cinema?
apartmen	apartment

Malay – English

api	fire
April	April
arak	alcohol
arak champagne	champagne
arnab	rabbit
asap	smoke
asing	separate; foreign
atap	roof
atau	or
Australia	Australia
awal	early
B	
bagaimana?	how?
bagasi	baggage; luggage
bagasi tangan	hand luggage
bagus	nice; well
bagus betul	it's very nice
bahan api	fuel
bahaya	danger
baik	fine, good (weather); kind
anda sangat baik	you're very kind
baiki	fix
boleh anda baiki?	can you fix it?
baju	clothes; dress
baju hujan	raincoat
baju mandi	swimsuit
baju sejuk	sweater
baju t	T-shirt
baju tidur	pyjamas
bakar	to burn; grilled
bakul	basket
balang	jar
baldi	bucket
balut	wrap
tolong balutkannya	please wrap it up
balutan	bandage
balutan	bandage
bandar	city; town
banjir	flood
bank	bank
bantal	pillow
bantuan kecemasan	first aid
banyak	a lot
banyak sangat	too much
berapa?	how many?
berapa banyak?	how much?
bapa	father
bapa saya	my father
bapa mertua saya	my father-in-law
bar	bar
barang kemas	jewellery
barangkali	probably
barat	west

Malay – English

Malay	English
barisan	queue
baru	new
bas	bus
bas menuju ke pantai	the bus to the beach
bas menuju ke pusat membeli-belah	the bus to the shopping centre
bas pertama	the first bus
boleh saya pergi dengan bas?	can I go by bus?
stesen bas	bus station
basah	wet
basi	rotten (food)
ini sudah basi	this is off (milk, food)
basikal	bicycle
batal	cancel
bateri	battery (for car)
baterinya sudah lemah	battery (for torch, camera)
saya perlukan bateri untuk ini	I need batteries for this
batuk	to cough
bau	smell
membau	to smell
bawa	to bring; to carry
bawang	onion
bawang putih	garlic
bayang-bayang	shade (shadow)
bayar	to pay
di mana patut saya bayar?	where do I pay?
bayar balik	to refund
saya mahu bayaran balik	I'd like a refund
bayaran masuk	admission charge
bayi	baby
bazar	bazaar
bebas cukai	duty free
beg	bag
beg galas	backpack
beg pakaian	suitcase
saya kehilangan beg pakaian	I've lost my suitcase
beg tangan	handbag
beg tidur	sleeping bag
bekas abu rokok	ashtray
beku	frozen
belakang	back (of body)
benang	thread
benar	true
itu benar	that's true
itu tidak benar	that's not true

Malay	English
bengkak	swollen (finger, ankle, etc.)
beracun	poisonous
berangin	windy;
beranginnya	it's windy
berasingan	separately
berat	heavy; weight
berbahaya	dangerous
berbaris	to queue
bercakap	to talk
bercerai	divorced
saya sudah bercerai	I'm divorced
berdarah	to bleed
berehat	to rest
berenang	to swim
adakah selamat untuk berenang?	is it safe to swim?
berfungsi	to work
ia tidak berfungsi	it doesn't work
berguna	useful
berharga	valuable
berhenti!	stop!
berita	news
berjalan	to walk
berjemur	sunbathe
berjumpa	to meet
berkahwin	married
anda sudah berkahwin?	are you married?
saya sudah berkahwin	I'm married
berkata	to say
apa anda kata?	what did you say?
tolong katakan lagi	please say that again
berkelah	picnic
berkhemah	to camp
berlanggar	crash (collision)
berlayar	sailing
berlepas	departures
berminyak	greasy
ia terlalu berminyak	it's too greasy (food)
bermula	to begin
bernafas	to breathe
bersama-sama	together
bersara	retired
bersih	clean
ia tak bersih	it's not clean
tolong bersihkan bilik air	please clean the bath
tolong bersihkan bilik saya	please clean my room
bertentangan dengan	opposite
bertuah	lucky

Malay – English

Malay - English

bertunang	engaged (to be married)	bidai	blinds (on window)	bilik mandi dengan pancuran	shower (bath)
bertutur	to speak	bil	bill	bilik menunggu	waiting room
anda boleh bertutur dalam bahasa Inggeris?	do you speak English?	tolong berikan saya bil	the bill, please	bilik salinan	changing room
		ada kesilapan dalam bil	there's a mistake on the bill	bilik tidur	bedroom
saya tak boleh bertutur dalam bahasa Melayu	I don't speak Malay	bila?	when?	bilik tiket	box office
		bilakah ia akan ditutup?	when does it close?	bintang	star
berus	brush	bilik	room	bir	beer
berus gigi	toothbrush	bilik air persendirian	private bathroom	sebotol bir	a bottle of beer
berus rambut	hairbrush	bilik bujang	single room	segelas bir	a glass of beer
besar	big	bilik kelamin	double room	biru	blue
besi	iron (metal)	bilik mandi	bathroom	biru laut	navy blue
betul	right (correct); real	bilik mandi dengan bilik mandi	bathroom with bathroom	bising	noisy
ini emas betul?	is it real gold?	di manakah bilik mandi?	where is the bathroom?	biskut	biscuits
ini kulit betul?	is it real leather?			bodoh	stupid
biasa	plain			bola	ball
				bola golf	golf ball
				bola lisut	volleyball
				bola sepak	football (game)
				bola tenis	tennis ball

Malay	English	Malay	English	Malay	English
boleh diharap	reliable (person, service)	saya bujang	I'm single	cadar	sheet (for bed)
bomba	fire brigade	buka	open	cair	weak (tea, coffee, drink)
bongkok/bengkok	to bend	ia sudah dibuka?	is it open?	caj perkhidmatan	service charge
bot	boat	buku	book	cantik	beautiful; pretty; lovely
bot penyelamat	lifeboat	buku cek	cheque book	cara	way (method)
botol	bottle	buku nota	notebook	cat kuku	nail polish
sebotol air	a bottle of water	bulan	month; moon	cawan	cup
brandi	brandy	bulan madu	honeymoon	CD	CD
buah	fruit	kami sedang berbulan madu	we're on honeymoon	anda ada CDnya?	do you have it on CD?
buah-buahan segar	fresh fruit	bunga	flower	cek	cheque
buah oren	orange	bunga api	fireworks	cek kembara	Travellers' Cheques
buatan tangan	handmade	bungkus	packet	cemerlang	excellent
budak lelaki	boy	buruk	bad	cenderamata	souvenir
budak perempuan	girl	burung	bird	cengkerang	shell
bujang	single (unmarried)	buta	blind (person)	cepat	fast; hurry
				cepat-cepat	quickly

C

cacar air — chickenpox

Malay - English

Malay – English

Malay	English
saya nak cepat	I'm in a hurry
ceri	cherry
cermin	mirror
cermin mata	sunglasses
gelap	
cerut	cigar
chop	chop (meat)
cincin	ring (for finger)
cincin perkahwinan	wedding ring
cip	chips
cirit-birit	diarrhoea
Coke®	Coke®
cokelat	chocolate
cokelat panas	hot chocolate
cuba	try on
boleh saya cuba?	can I try it on?
cuci kereta	car wash
cukai	tax; VAT
cukup	enough

Malay	English
ia tak cukup	it's not enough
cukup masak	well done (meat)
curam	steep
curam kah?	is it steep?
cuti	holiday
cuti umum	public holiday
D	
dada	chest (of body)
dadah	drug (recreational)
daftar masuk	to check in
pada pukul berapa patut saya daftar masuk?	what time should I check in?
daging	beef, meat
daging babi	ham; pork
daging babi mentah	raw ham
daging rusa	veal

Malay	English
dahulu	ago
dalam	deep
dan	and
dapur	kitchen
dapur masak	cooker
darah	blood
daripada	from
datang	to come (arrive)
datuk	grandfather
dekat	close; near
dekat tak?	is it close by?
dekat kah?	is it near?
demam	temperature (fever)
demam selsema	flu
saya demam	I have a temperature
denda	fine (to be paid)
dengan	by; with
dengan bas	by bus
dengan kereta	by car

Malay	English
dengan keretapi	by train
denyar	flash (for camera)
deodoran	deodorant
depan	front
deposit	deposit
desa	country (not town)
detergen	detergent
dewasa	adult
di	at (place)
di atas	above
di bawah	below
di belakang	behind
di hadapan	ahead
di mana?	where?
di mana boleh saya beli roti?	where can I buy bread?
di mana boleh saya tukar wang?	where can I change money?
di manakah bank?	where is the bank?
di manakah perhentian bas?	where is the bus stop?
di sebelah	beside; next to
di sebelah kanan	on/to the right
di sini	here
di tingkat atas	upstairs
di tingkat bawah	downstairs
dia	he; she
diari	diary
diet	diet
saya sedang berdiet	I'm on a diet
dilarang	forbidden
dilarang berkhemah	no camping
dilarang menawar	no bargaining
dilarang merokok	non-smoking
direbus *(makanan)*	boiled (food)
direktori telefon	telephone directory
disel	diesel
di mana boleh saya dapatkan disel?	where can I get diesel?
Disember	December
disengat	stung
Saya telah disengat	I've been stung
diskaun	discount
disko	disco
ditempah	reserved
doktor	doctor
doktor gigi	dentist

Malay – English

Malay	English
dokumen	documents
di manakah dokumen itu?	where are the documents?
dompet	wallet
dozen	dozen
dua hala	return (ticket)
duduk	sit
boleh saya duduk di depan?	can I sit in the front?
duit	money
duit syiling	change (loose coins)
duit tip	tip (to waiter, etc.)
mana duit baki saya?	where's my change?
tali pinggang duit	money belt

E

Malay	English
eja	spell
bagaimana hendak mengejanya?	how do you spell it?
ejen	agent
ejen hartanah	estate agent
ejen pelancongan	travel agent
elektrik	electric
emas	gold
e-mel	e-mail
enak	delicious
enaknya!	this is delicious!
England	England
enjin	engine
epal	apple
Eropah	Europe
esok	tomorrow
pagi esok	tomorrow morning

F

Malay	English
petang esok	tomorrow evening
faham	understand
anda faham?	do you understand?
saya tak faham	I don't understand
Febuari	February
feri	ferry
fesyen	fashion
filem	film
flat (apartmen)	flat (apartment)
folder	folder
fotograf	photograph
fotokopi	photocopy

G

Malay	English
galeri (lukisan)	art gallery
gambar	picture (on wall)

Malay	English		
garam	salt	gigi palsu	dentures
garpu	fork (for eating)	gigitan	bite (insect, dog)
gas	gas	gigitan serangga	insect bite
gatal	itch	gincu	lipstick
gaun	dress	golf	golf
gedung serba ada	department store	goreng	fried (food)
gelang elastik	elastic band	gua	cave
gelanggang tenis	tennis court	gula	sugar
gelap	dark	gula-gula	sweets
gelas	glass (for drink)	gula-gula getah	chewing gum
segelas air	a glass of water	gula-gula pudina	mints
segelas wain	a glass of wine	gunting	scissors
gembira	happy	gunting rambut	haircut
gempa bumi	earthquake	gunung	mountain
gemuk	fat (person)	guru	teacher
gereja	church		
get	gate		
getah	rubber		
gigi	tooth; teeth		

H

habis dijual	sold out
habuk	dust
hadiah	gift ; present
ini hadiah	this is a present
halaman	garden
hamil	pregnant
saya hamil	I'm pregnant
hangat	warm
hanya	only
harga	price
hari	day
hari ini	today
hari lahir	birthday
Hari Krismas	Christmas
setiap hari	every day
harian	daily
hati-hati	caution
haus	thirsty
saya haus	I'm thirsty
helo	hello

herba - kad

Malay – English

Malay	English
herba	herbs
hiburan	entertainment
hidangan utama	main course (of meal)
hidung	nose
hidup	on
hijau	green
hilang	lost; missing (thing)
dompet saya hilang	my wallet is missing
hiris	slice
hitam	black
hodoh	ugly
hospital	hospital
tolong pergi ke hospital	to the hospital, please
hotel	hotel
hujan	rain
hutan	forest
hutang	to owe

I

Malay	English
ia	it
ibu	mother
ibu bapa	parents
ibu mertua	mother-in-law
ikan	fish
ikan segar	fresh fish
ingat	to remember
Inggeris	English
boleh bertutur dalam bahasa Inggeris?	do you speak English?
saya orang Inggeris	I'm English
ini	this; these

anda perlu bayar saya ... — you owe me ...
berapa perlu saya bayar? — what do I owe you?

Malay	English
boleh saya beli ini?	can I buy this?
insuran	insurance
termasuk insuran?	is insurance included?
invois	invoice
Ireland	Ireland
Ireland Utara	Northern Ireland
isih	sort (type)
Isnin	Monday
istana	castle; palace
isteri	wife
istimewa	special
Itali	Italy
itu	that; those

J

Malay	English
jadi	to happen
apa telah terjadi?	what happened?
jadual waktu	timetable

jaket	jacket
jaket	life jacket
keselamatan	
jaket kulit	leather jacket
jalan	route; way; road
apakah jalan	what's the best
terbaik?	route?
ini jalan yang	is this the right
betul?	way?
inilah jalan	is this the road
yang menuju	to...?
ke...?	
jalan keluar	way out
jam	clock; hour
dalam masa	in an hour's
sejam	time
jam penggera	alarm clock
jam tangan	watch (wrist)
jamin	guarantee
jangkitan	infection
jantung	heart

serangan	heart attack
jantung	
Januari	January
jarum	needle
jarum dan	a needle and
benang	thread
jatuh	to fall
jauh	far
berapa	how far is the
jauhkah	beach?
pantai?	
jauhkah?	is it far?
jawapan	answer
takda	there's no
jawapan	answer (phone)
jem	jam (food)
jenaka	joke
jenis darah	blood group
Jerman	Germany
jingga	orange (colour)
jiran	neighbour

jualan	sale
Julai	July
Jumaat	Friday
jumlah	total
Jun	June
jurujual	salesperson
jururawat	nurse
jus	juice
jus buah	fruit juice
jus epal	apple juice
jus oren	orange juice
jus tomato	tomato juice

K

kabus	fog
kacang	nuts (nibbles)
kacang tanah	peanuts
kad	card
kad hari lahir	birthday card
kad kredit	credit card

Malay – English

Malay – English

Malay	English
saya kehilangan	I've lost my
kad kredit	credit card
kad pengenalan	identification card
kad telefon	phonecard
kadang-kadang	sometimes
kadar	rate
kadar pertukaran	exchange rate
kafe	café
kakak	elder sister
kaki	foot; leg
kalis air	waterproof
kamera	camera
kamera video	camcorder
kami	we; our
kami terhibur	we had a nice time
kampung	village
kamus	dictionary

Malay	English
kanak-kanak	child
kanta lekap	contact lens
saya kehilangan kanta lekap	I've lost my contact lenses
kapal	ship
kapal pesiar	yacht
kapalterbang	aeroplane
kapas (kain)	cotton (material)
kain kapas kah?	is it cotton?
kastam	customs
kasut	shoes
kasut but	boots
katil	bed
katil budak	cot; crib
katil kelamin	double bed
katil kembar	twin beds
kaunter	counter (desk)
kawalan kastam	customs control

Malay	English
kawan	friend
kaya	rich (person)
kayu	wood (substance)
kayu golf	golf club
ke	to
ke stesen	to the station
ke depan	forward(s)
kecemasan	emergency
pintu keluar kecemasan	emergency exit
kecil	little; small
kedai	shop
kedai buku	bookshop
kedai cenderamata	souvenir shop
kedai farmasi malam	chemist's night duty
ahli farmasi	chemist
di mana ahli farmasi?	where is the chemist?

Malay – English

Malay	English
kedai hadiah	gift shop
kedai kek	cake shop
kedai muzik	music shop
kedai penjual daging	butcher's
kedai penjual sayur	greengrocer's
kedai runcit	grocer's
kedai tukang buat roti	baker's
kediaman	home
kedua	second
tiket kelas kedua	a second-class ticket
kedua-duanya	both
saya hendak kedua-duanya	I'd like both
kedutaan	embassy
kedutaan Amerika	American Embassy
kedutaan British	British Embassy
kegemaran	favourite
keju	cheese
kek	cake
kelab malam	nightclub
kelabu	grey
kelajuan	speed
kelajuan maksimum	maximum speed
kelambu	mosquito net
kelapa	coconut
kelas kedua	second class
kelas pertama	first class
keluar	out; to go out
dia sudah keluar	he's gone out
keluarga	family
keluarga saya	my family
kemalangan	accident
kembali	to return
kembar	twins
kemeja	shirt
kenapa	why
kepala	head
kepincangan	fault (defect)
keping	piece (slice)
kepunyaan siapa	whose
ini kepunyaan siapa?	whose is it?
kerang-kerangan	shellfish
saya tak makan kerang-kerangan	I don't eat shellfish
kerap	frequent; often
kereta	car
kereta automatik	automatic car
kereta sorong	pushchair

Malay – English

Malay	English
keretapi	train
stesen keretapi	railway station
kering	dry
kerosakan	damage
kertas	paper
kertas kesat	napkin
kertas tulisan	writing paper
kerusi	chair; seat
kerusi kereta budak	car seat (for child)
kerusi khas	reserved seat
kerusi malas	deck chair
kerusi roda	wheelchair
kerusi tinggi budak	high chair
ketat	tight
ia terlalu ketat	it's too tight
ketibaan	arrivals
ketinggalan	to miss (plane, train, etc.)
saya ketinggalan (bas, keretapi, kapalterbang)	I missed my (bus, train, plane)
saya ketinggalan penyambung	connection
saya ketinggalan bas	I missed the bus
ketinggian	height
ketuhar	oven
ketuhar gelombang mikro	microwave (oven)
ketuk (knock)	tap (knock)
kewarganegaraan	nationality
Khamis	Thursday
khemah	tent
khidmat	service
khidmat bilik	room service
khidmat dobi	laundry service
kilang	factory
kipas	fan
kiri	left
kismis	raisins
kocek	pocket
kod pendailan	dialling code
koko	cocoa
kolam	pool
kolam renang	swimming pool
ada tak kolam?	is there a pool?
kompas	compass
komputer	computer
kondom	condoms
konsert	concert
konsert pop	pop concert
konsulat	consulate
konsulat Amerika	American Consulate

konsulat	British
British	Consulate
kopi	coffee
kopi o	black coffee
kopi nyahkafeina	decaffeinated coffee
kopi o ais	iced coffee
kopi segera	instant coffee
kos	cost
berapa kosnya?	how much does it cost?
kosong	empty; zero; free (unoccupied); vacancy (room)
kot	coat
kotak	box
kotor	dirty
krim (tenusu)	cream (dairy)
krim pencukuran	shaving cream

kualiti	quality
kualiti bagus	good quality
kualiti buruk	poor quality
kuat	loud
kucing	cat
kuda	horse
kuilt	quilt
kulit	leather; skin
kumpulan	group (of people)
kunci	key; lock
saya terlupa kunci saya	I've forgotten my key
kunci saya	my key
tolong berikan saya kunci	my key, please
kuning	yellow
kunjungan	trip
kunjungan sehari	a day trip
kurang masak	rare (steak)
kurang upaya	disabled (person)

kurus	thin
kusyen	cushion

L

laci	drawer
lada hitam	pepper (spice)
ladang	farm
lagi	more
lagi...	some more...
lagu	song
lain	other; different
lama	long
berapa lama?	how long will it take?
lambai	wave (hand)
lambat	late
maaf, saya lambat	sorry I'm late
lampu	lamp; light (illumination)
lampu trafik	traffic lights

Malay – English

Malay – English

langit	sky	lebuh raya	motorway
lantai	floor	lecuh	blister
lapangan terbang	airport	leher	neck
lapar	hungry	lelah	asthma
saya lapar	I'm hungry	lelaki	man
laut	sea	lemas	to drown
saya rasa mabuk laut	I'm feeling seasick	lembut	soft
lawatan	tour	lengan	arm
lawatan berpandu	guided tour	lengan saya sakit	my arm hurts
lebah	bee	lesen	licence (driving)
lebih	more	lesen memandu	driving licence
lebih baik (daripada)	better (than)	liat	tough (meat)
lebih besar	bigger; larger	lif	lift (elevator)
lebih kecil	smaller	lilin	candle
lebih suka	to prefer	linen	linen
saya lebih suka teh	I'd prefer tea	lintasan pejalan kaki	pedestrian crossing
		lipas	cockroach
		lobak	radish

loker	locker (for luggage)		
longkang	drain		
losyen	lotion		
losyen pelindung matahari	suntan lotion		
loya	sick		
saya rasa loya	I feel sick		
lumba (sukan)	race (sport)		
lukisan	painting (picture)		
luncur air	water-skiing		
luput	to expire		
lutut	knee		

M

maaf	sorry
maaf!	pardon!
maafkan saya!	excuse me!
minta maaf!	I'm sorry!

mabuk	drunk	matahari	sun
saya mabuk	I'm drunk	mawar	rose
mabuk laut	seasick	Mei	May
Mac	March	meja	table
madu	honey	meja	enquiry desk
mahal	expensive	*pertanyaan*	
ini terlalu	it's too	*meja tunai*	cash desk
mahal	expensive	melancong	to travel
main	to play	melarikan diri	escape
anda boleh	do you play	melawat	to visit
main tenis?	tennis?	melekat	stuck
mainan	toy	*ia melekat*	it's stuck
majlis	party	meletak kereta	to park
	(celebration)	meluncur	surfing
majlis	town hall	memadamkan	to switch off
bandaran			(radio, light)
makan malam	dinner (evening	memakai	to wear
	meal)	memakan	to eat
makan	lunch	memanas	heating
tengahari		memancing	to fish
makanan	food; meal	memandu	to drive
makanan bayi	baby food		
makanan	delicatessen		
istimewa			
makanan laut	seafood		
makcik	aunt		
maklumat	information		
maksud	mean		
apa	what does it		
maksudnya?	mean?		
malam	night		
malam ini	tonight		
semalam	last night		
mancis	matches (light)		
mandi	bath		
manis	sweet		
marah	angry		
saya marah	I'm angry		
masjid	mosque		
masuk!	come in!		
mata	eye		

Malay – English

Malay – English

Malay	English
memasak	to cook
memasuki	to enter; to get into
membaca	to read (*book, etc.*)
membaiki	to repair
membakar	to burn
membasuh	to wash
membeli	to buy
membeli-belah	shopping
membenarkan	to let (*allow*)
memberi	to give
memberi laluan	give way
membersihkan	to clean
membosankan	boring
ia membosankan	it's boring
membuang sampah	litter (*rubbish*)
membuat	to make
membuka	to open
memecahkan	to break
memesan	to order (*food*)
memikir	to think
meminjamkan	to lend
memotong	to cut
memotong	to overtake
mempercayai	to believe
saya tak percayakan anda	I don't believe you
memulakan	to start
bilakah ia akan bermula?	when does it start?
menahan	to arrest
menaiki	to get on board
menandatangani	to sign (*form, cheque, etc.*)
menangis	to cry (*weep*)
menari	to dance
menarik	attractive; interesting; to pull
menawar	bargain
mencari	to find; to look for
mencium	to kiss
mencukur	to shave
mendaki	climbing; to go climbing
mendapat	to get
mendarat	to land
kapalterbang sudah mendarat?	has the plane landed?
mendengar	to hear; to listen to
menelefon	to call (*on phone*)
boleh saya menelefon dari sini?	can I phone from here?

Malay	English	Malay	English	Malay	English
menempah	to reserve (room, table, etc.)	mengemas	to pack (bags)	mengupah, menyewa	to hire
menerangkan	to explain	mengembara	to hitchhike	(rent)	be
sila terangkan	please explain	tumpang		menjadi	
menerima	to accept	mengepos	to post	menjaga	to look after
menetap	to live	mengesahkan	to confirm		someone
saya menetap di London	I live in London	mengetahui	to know	menjawab	to answer
		saya tahu	I know	menjual	to sell
mengambil	to take	saya tak tahu	I don't know	menolak	to push
boleh anda ambil gambar kami?	will you take a picture of us?	menggeluncur	to skate	menolong	to help
		menggunakan	to use	membantu	can you help
		menghantar	to send	boleh anda bantu saya?	me?
boleh saya ambil gambar?	can I take pictures?	menghendaki	to want	mentega	butter
mengganggur	unemployed	menghidupkan	to switch on	menterjemah	to translate
mengapa	why	menghidupkan	to turn on	mentol (lampu)	bulb (light)
mengayuh	to cycle (bicycle)	menginap	to stay	menu	menu
mengekori	to follow	saya menginap di Hotel...	I'm staying at the...Hotel	tolong bawa menu	the menu, please
lelaki itu	that man is	mengisi	to fill (up)	menukar	to change (money)
mengekori saya	following me	mengulang	to repeat		
		mengunci	to lock		
		mengundang	to invite		

Malay – English

Malay – English

Malay	English
menulis	to write
menunaikan	to cash
menunggu	to wait (for)
sila tunggu	please wait
menunjuk	to show
menutup	to close; to shut
menyakitkan	painful
ia sangat menyakitkan	it's very painful
menyalin (fotokopi)	to copy (photocopy)
menyayangi	to love (to really like)
menyebut	to pronounce
bagaimana hendak menyebut ini?	how is this pronounced?
menyelam	to dive
menyerang	to attack
menyeronok-kan	exciting
menyewa	to rent
saya mahu menyewa kereta	I want to hire a car
menyimpan	to keep
menyintai	to love (romantically)
aku cinta pada mu	I love you
merah	red
merah jambu	pink
mereka	they
merokok	to smoke
saya tidak merokok	I don't smoke
tolong jangan merokok	please don't smoke
mesin basuh	washing machine
mesin penjawab	answering machine
mesyuarat	meeting
meter (teksi)	meter (taxi)
minggu	week
hari minggu	weekend
minggu depan	next week
minggu lepas	last week
minit	minute
minum	to drink
minuman	drink
minuman bergas	soft drink
minyak	oil
minyak wangi	perfume
minyak zaitun	olive oil
misai	moustache
miskin	poor (not rich)
mudah	easy
muka	face
mulut	mouth
mungkin	possible

Malay	English
ia tidak mungkin	it's impossible
murah	cheap
saya hendak yang paling murah	I want the cheapest
musim panas	summer
dalam musim panas	in summer
Muslim	Muslim
mustahak	important
mustard	mustard
mutiara	pearl
muzium	museum

N

Malay	English
nama	name
apa nama anda?	what's your name?
nama bapa	surname
nama saya ...	my name is ...
nanti	later
nasi	rice (cooked)
nelayan	fisherman
nenek	grandmother
New Zealand	New Zealand
nombor	number
nombor telefon	phone number
November	November
nyamuk	mosquitoes

O

Malay	English
Ogos	August
OK	OK
Oktober	October
ombak (sea)	wave
operator	operator (telephone)
orang	person
orang Amerika	American
orang Australia	Australian
orang British	British
saya orang British	I'm British
orang Ireland	Irish
orang Itali	Italian
orang Jerman	German
orang Scotland	Scottish

P

Malay	English
pada	at (time)
padam	off (radio, engine, etc.)
padan	to fit
ia tak padan dengan saya	it doesn't fit me
pagi	morning
pada waktu pagi	in the morning
pagi esok	tomorrow morning
pagi ini	this morning
pahit	bitter (taste)

Malay – English

Malay	English
pai	pie
paip	pipe (for smoking); tap (faucet)
pakaian	clothes
pakaian dalam	underwear
pakar optik	optician
pakcik	uncle
pakej pelancongan	package tour
paku	nail (metal)
palam	plug (electric)
pameran	exhibition
panas	hot
ia terlalu panas	it's too hot
panduan (buku panduan)	guide/guidebook
panggilan (telefon)	telephone call
panggilan pindah bayaran	reverse-charge call
panggilan antarabangsa	international call
panggung	theatre
panggung wayang	cinema
di manakah panggung wayang?	where is the cinema?
pantai	beach; coast
papan luncur	surfboard
para	shelf
pas masuk	boarding card
pasang	pair
pasangan	couple (two people)
pasangan saya	my partner (in couple)
pasar raya	supermarket
pasir	sand
pasport	passport
pasta	pasta
pasukan	team (football)
patung	doll
payung	sunshade; umbrella
pecah	broken
pedas	spicy
peguam	lawyer
pejabat	office
saya kerja di sebuah pejabat	I work in an office
pejabat maklumat	information office
pejabat pelancong	tourist office
pejabat pos	post office
di manakah pejabat pos?	where is the post office?

Malay	English	Malay	English	Malay	English
pejabat simpan bagasi	left-luggage office	*pemanis*	sweetener	*pencabut*	tweezers
pejabat tiket	ticket office	*pembantu kedai*	shop assistant	*pencabut gabus*	corkscrew
pejalan kaki	pedestrian	*pembantu rumah*	maid	*pencuci hampagas*	vacuum cleaner
pekak	deaf	*pembasmi kuman*	disinfectant	*pencuci kanta lekap*	contact lens cleaner
pekat	strong (tea, coffee)	*pembersih cat kuku*	nail polish remover	*pencuci kering*	dry cleaner's
pekerjaan	job	*pembuka botol*	bottle opener	*pencuci mulut*	dessert
apa pekerjaan anda?	what's your job?	*pembuka tin*	can opener	*pencukur*	shaver
pelabuhan	port (harbour)	*pemetik api*	lighter (cigarette)	*pencuri*	thief
peladang	farmer	*anda ada pemetik api?*	do you have a light?	*pendandan rambut*	hairdresser
pelancong	tourist	*pen*	pen	*pendek*	short
pelawat	visitor	*penangguhan*	delay	*penempahan*	reservation
pelayan	waiter/waitress	*ada penangguhan kah?*	is there a delay?	*saya hendak membatalkan penempahan saya*	I want to cancel my booking
pelukis	artist	*penat*	tired	*saya telah menempah*	I've booked
pemadam api	fire extinguisher			*penerbangan*	flight
pemain CD	CD player				
pemandangan	view				
pemandu	driver				

Malay - English

Malay	English
penerbangan terus	direct flight
pengasuh	babysitter
pengering rambut	hair dryer
penggeluncur	skates
penggera	alarm
penggera api	fire alarm
penghawa dingin	air conditioning
penghidap kencing manis	diabetic
pengilat	polish (for shoes)
pengsan	to faint
pengurus	manager
pengusir serangga	insect repellent
pening	dizzy
penisilin	penicillin
penkek	pancake
pensel	pencil

Malay	English
penterjemah	interpreter
penting	urgent
ia penting	it's urgent
penuh	full
isi sampai penuh!	fill it up!
penumpang	passenger
penuntut	student
penyakit	disease
penyakit anjing gila	rabies
penyambung (keretapi, kapal terbang)	connection (train, plane)
penyelamat lemas	lifeguard
penyengat	wasp
perabot	furniture
perak	silver
ini perak kah?	is it silver?

Malay	English
peralatan tempat tidur	bedclothes
peralatan tempat tidur ini kotor	these bedclothes are dirty
saya perlukan peralatan tempat tidur lagi	I need more bedclothes
Perancis	French
perang	brown; war
perapi	conditioner (for hair)
peraturan	regulations
percuma	nothing (no cost)
pergi	away; to leave; to go
kami akan berangkat esok	we leave tomorrow

Malay	English
tolong pergi dari sini!	please go away!
perhatian	attention
perhentian bas	bus stop
periksa	check
perisa	flavour
periuk	pot (for cooking)
perjalanan	journey
perjalanan bot	boat trip
perkahwinan	wedding
perkataan	word
perlahan	slow
perlawanan	match (game)
perlu	to be necessary; to need
perlu tempah kah?	is it necessary to book?
saya perlu berangkat	I need to go
saya perlu berehat	I need to rest
saya perlu sebuah kereta	I need a car
permaidani	carpet; rug
permainan (sukan)	game (sport)
permaisuri	queen
permata	diamond
permit	permit
saya perlu permit kah?	do I need a permit?
perniagaan	business
persembahan	performance
persendirian	private
persidangan	conference
pertama	first
keretapi pertama	the first train
perut	stomach
pesanan	message
ada apa-apa pesanan?	are there any messages?
peta	map
peta jalan	road map; street map
petang	evening
makanan petang	evening meal
petang esok	tomorrow evening
petang ini	this evening
peti ais	freezer
peti besi	safe
peti sejuk	fridge
peti surat	postbox
petrol	petrol
petrol tanpa plumbum	unleaded petrol
pil	pill
pil perancang	contraceptive pill
pil tidur	sleeping pill
pil vitamin	vitamin pills

Malay – English

Malay	English
pin	pin
pin dawai	safety pin
ping pong	table tennis
pinggan	plate
pintu	door
pintu depan	front door
pintu kecemasan	fire exit
pintu keluar	exit
di manakah pintu keluar?	where is the exit?
pintu masuk	entrance
di manakah pintu masuk?	where is the entrance?
pisau	knife
pisau cukur	razor
pisau cukur elektrik	electric razor
pita (cassette)	tape (cassette)
plastik	plastic

Malay	English
platform	platform (railway)
plet nombor	number plate
pokok	tree
polis	police
pondok telefon	telephone box
poskad	postcard
poskod	postcode (zip code)
poster	poster
potong	cut
preskripsi	prescription
puding	pudding
pulang	to go back
pulau	island
pusat	central
pusat bandar	city/town centre
putih	white

R

Malay	English
Rabu	Wednesday
radio	radio
rakan niaga	partner (business)
raket tenis	tennis racket
ramalan	forecast (weather)
ramalan cuaca	weather forecast
rambut	hair
rantai	chain
rasa	feel
saya rasa loya	I feel sick
saya rasa penat	I feel tired
saya rasa pening	I feel dizzy
saya rasa tidak sihat	I don't feel well
rasa	taste

Malay – English

Malay	English
boleh saya rasa sedikit?	can I taste some?
rata	flat
resipi	recipe
resit	receipt
restoran	restaurant
ribut	storm
risalah	brochure
rokok	cigarettes
sekotak rokok	a packet of cigarettes
rompakan	burglary
rosak	broken down (car, machine); out of order; to break down
roti	bread
anda jual roti?	do you sell bread?
tolong berikan saya roti lagi	more bread, please
roti bakar	toast
ruam (skin)	rash (skin)
ruang makan	dining room
rumah	house
rumah tumpangan	guesthouse
S	
Sabtu	Saturday
sabun	soap
sah	valid
saiz	size (shoes)
saiz lebih besar	bigger size
saiz lebih kecil	smaller size
sakit	ache; hurt
sakit gigi	toothache
sakit kepala	headache
sakit telinga	earache
saya sakit telinga	I have earache
salad	salad
salad kentang	potato salad
salad tomato	tomato salad
salah	wrong
salin	copy
salmon	salmon
saluran	pipe (drain, etc.)
sama	same
sampul	envelope
sandal	sandals
sangat	very
sangat baik	very good
saran	to recommend
sarapan pagi	breakfast
pada pukul berapa?	what time is
sarapan pagi	breakfast?
termasuk	included
sarapan pagi	breakfast included
sardin	sardines
satu	a(n); single (one); one

Malay – English

Malay	English
hanya satu	only one
satu lagi	another
satu lagi bir	another beer
saudara	relation (family member)
saya	I
saya sibuk	I'm busy
sayur	vegetable
sayur-sayuran	fresh vegetables
segar	fresh
Scotland	Scotland
saya orang Scotland	I'm Scottish
sebelum	before
sebelum makan malam	before dinner
sebelum pukul 4	before 4 o'clock
sebenar	genuine
sedang	landing
mendarat	

Malay	English
sedap	tasty
sedih	sad
sedikit	a little bit; few
tolong berikan saya sedikit sahaja	just a little, please
segar	fresh
ia segar kah?	is it fresh?
sejuk	to be cold
saya sejuk	I'm cold
saya mahu minuman sejuk	I'd like a cold drink
sekali	once
sekali lagi	again
sekarang	now
sekarang juga	at once
sekolah	school
selalunya	usually
selama-lamanya	forever

Malay	English
selamat	safe
selamat!	cheers!
selamat datang	welcome!
selamat hari lahir!	happy birthday!
selamat jalan	goodbye
selamat malam	goodnight
selamat siang	good day
Selasa	Tuesday
selatan	south
selekeh	dinghy
selekoh	bend
selepas	after
selesa	comfortable
selimut	blanket
selipar	slippers
selsema	cold (illness)
saya menghidap selsema	I have a cold

Malay	English	Malay	English	Malay	English
seluar	trousers (pants)	serangan	attack	bilakah bot yang seterusnya?	when is the next boat?
seluar jean	jeans	serangan jantung	heart attack	setiap	every; per
seluar pendek	shorts (short trousers)	serangga	insect	setiap hari	every day
seluruh	whole	serbuk pencuci	washing powder	setiap tahun	every year
semalam	yesterday	serius	serious	setiap jam	per hour
sementara	temporary	seriuskah?	is it serious?	setiap kilometer	per kilometre
sempit	narrow	serta-merta	immediately	setiap minggu	per week; weekly
sempurna	perfect	seseorang	someone	setiap orang	everyone; per person
ia sempurna	it's perfect	sesetengah	some	sewa	rent
semua	all	sesuatu	something	berapa sewanya?	how much is the rent?
semut	ants	setem	stamp	siap	ready
senarai harga	price list	setengah	half	sudah siap?	is it ready?
sendiri	alone	setengah botol	half bottle	siapa	who
sentiasa	always	setengah jam	half an hour	sibuk	busy
senyap	quiet	seterika	iron (for clothes)	sijil	certificate
senyum	smile	seterusnya	next		
September	September	bilakah bas yang seterusnya?	when is the next bus?		
serang	to attack				
saya telah diserang	I've been attacked				

Malay – English

Malay	English
sikat	comb
silap	mistake
simpan	keep the
bakinya	change
sinki	sink; basin
skirt	skirt
soalan	question
sos	sauce
sosej	sausage
sotong	octopus; squid
span	sponge (for cleaning)
stadium	stadium
stesen	station
stesen bas	bus station
stesen petrol	petrol station
stesen polis	police station
stesen utama	central station
stokin	socks
straw	straw (for drinking)
suami	husband
suami saya	my husband
sudah bayar	paid
saya sudah bayar	I've already paid
sudah ditutup	closed
sudu	spoon
sudut	corner
suhu	temperature
berapa suhunya?	what is the temperature?
suka	to like; to enjoy
saya suka	I enjoy
saya suka berenang	swimming
main tenis	I enjoy playing tennis
sukan	sport
sungai	river
sup	soup
suratkhabar	newspaper
susah	difficult
susu	milk
di mana boleh	where can I buy
saya beli susu?	milk?
susu segar	fresh milk
susu skim	skimmed milk
susu tepung	powdered milk
sut	suit (clothes)
sutera	silk
ini sutera kah?	is it silk?
syampu	shampoo
syarikat	company (business)
syiling	coin

T

Malay	English
tahniah!	congratulations!
tahun	year
Tahun Baru	New Year
tahun ini	this year
saya berumur ... tahun	I'm ... years old

Malay	English
tak ada	none
tak ada	nothing
apa-apa	
tak apa-apa	alright (OK)
anda tak apa-apa?	are you all right?
Saya tak apa-apa	I'm all right
tak bernasib baik	unlucky
tak lama lagi	soon
tak selesa	uncomfortable
tali	rope; string
tali leher	tie
tali pinggang	belt
tali pinggang keledar	seat belt
taman	park
tamat	finish
bilakah ia akan tamat?	when does it finish?

Malay	English
tambahan	extra; supplement
tambang	fare (train, bus, etc.)
berapakah tambangnya?	how much is the fare?
tanah perkuburan	cemetery
tanda	sign (road, notice, etc.)
tandas	toilet
tandas wanita	ladies' (toilet)
tandatangan	signature
tangan	hand
tangga	stairs
tangga kecemasan	fire escape
tanpa	without
tanpa alkohol	non-alcoholic
minuman tanpa alkohol	a non-alcoholic drink

Malay	English
tanpa karbonat	still (not fizzy)
tapak perkhemahan	camp site
tapis	filter
tarian	dance
tarikh (kalendar)	date (calendar)
apa tarikh hari ini?	what is the date?
tarikh lahir	date of birth
tasik	lake
teh	tea
teh o ais	iced tea
tekanan darah	blood pressure
tekanan darah tinggi	high blood pressure
teksi	taxi
telefon	phone
televisyen	television
telinga	ear

Malay – English

Malay – English

Malay	English	Malay	English	Malay	English
telur	egg	tepung	flour	tersekat	blocked
teman lelaki	boyfriend	terbaik	best	*sinki tersekat*	the sink is blocked
teman wanita	girlfriend	terbakar	burnt	terup	cards (*playing*)
tempah	to book	terbang	to fly	terus	direct
tempat letak kereta	car park	terbesar	biggest	*ini keretapi terus kah?*	is it a direct train?
tempat menyambut tetamu	reception (*desk*)	tercedera	injured	terus	straight on
		Saya tercedera	I've been injured	jalan terus	keep straight on
tengah	middle	teres	terrace	terus di hadapan	straight ahead
tengah malam	midnight	terima kasih	thank you	tetamu	guest
tengahari	afternoon; midday	tak apa, terima kasih	no, thanks	tetanus	tetanus
pada waktu tengahari	in the afternoon	terjaga	to wake up	tiba	to arrive
tengahari ini	this afternoon	terkena selaran matahari	sunburn	tidak	not; no
esok	tomorrow			*tidak hadam*	indigestion
tengahari	afternoon	terkenal	famous	*tidak mungkin*	impossible
tengok	to see	terlupa	to forget	*tidak pernah*	never
tenis	tennis	termasuk	included	tidur	to sleep
tentang	about	terowong	tunnel	tiket	ticket
		terpakai	secondhand	*tiket dua hala*	return ticket

Malay	English
tiket sehala	single ticket
tikus	mouse; rat
timun	cucumber
timur	east
tin	can (*tin*)
setin minyak	a can of oil
tinggi	high; tall
tingkap	window
tingkat pertama	first floor
tisu	tissues
tisu tandas	toilet paper
tidak ada tisu tandas	there is no toilet
tol	toll (*on motorway, etc.*)
tolong	please
tolong berikan saya roti	some bread, please
tolong!	help!
tomato	tomato
tong	bin (*for rubbish*)
tongkat	walking stick
topi	hat
topi keledar	crash helmet
tradisional	traditional
trafik	traffic
trak	truck
tua	elderly
tuala	towel (*hand towel*)
tuan punya	owner
tukang gunting rambut	barber
tukang paip	plumber
tukar	exchange
kadar pertukaran	exchange rate
tulang	bone
tuna	tuna
tunai	cash
saya tak ada wang tunai	I have no cash
tunang	fiancé(e)
tunjuk	show
tuntutan bagasi	baggage reclaim
turun	to get off (*bus, etc.*)
tutup	shut
sudah ditutup kah?	is it closed?

U

ubat	medicine
ubat gigi	toothpaste
ubat tahan sakit	painkiller
ubi kentang	potato
ubi kentang goreng	fried potatoes

Malay – English

ubi kentang lenyek	mashed potato	
ubi kentang rebus	boiled potatoes	
ubur-ubur	jellyfish	
udang	prawn; shrimp	
ukiran	sculpture	
ukur	measure	
boleh saya ukurkannya?	can I measure it?	
ular	snake	
umur	age; old	
berapa umur anda?	how old are you?	
ungu	purple	
universiti	university	
untuk	for	
untuk dijual	for sale	
untuk saya	for me	
usia	age	

berapa usianya?	how old is it? (building, etc.)	
utara	north	
uzur	ill	
saya uzur	I'm ill	

V

van	van	
vegetarian	vegetarian	
visa	visa	

W

wain	wine	
sebotol wain	a bottle of wine	
senarai wain	wine list	
wain merah	red wine	
wain putih	white wine	
waktu	time	
waktu buka	opening hours	
wanita	woman	
warga tua	senior citizen	

warna	colour	
wartawan	journalist	

X

X-ray	x-ray	

Y

ya	yes	
Yahudi	Jewish	
saya orang Yahudi	I'm Jewish	
yang mana?	which?	
platform yang mana?	which platform?	
yang mana satu?	which one?	
yuran masuk	entrance fee	

Z

zaitun	olives	
zoo	zoo	

Further titles in Collins' phrasebook range
Collins Gem Phrasebook

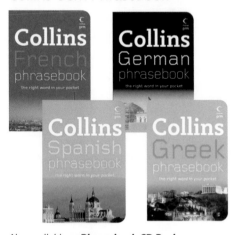

Also available as **Phrasebook CD Pack**
Other titles in the series

Afrikaans	Japanese	Portuguese
Arabic	Korean	Russian
Cantonese	Latin American	Thai
Croatian	Spanish	Turkish
Czech	Malay	Vietnamese
Dutch	Mandarin	Xhosa
Italian	Polish	Zulu

Collins Phrasebook and Dictionary

Other titles in the series
Greek Japanese Mandarin Polish Portuguese
Spanish Turkish

Collins Easy: Photo Phrasebook

Also available a
**Phrasebool
CD Pac**

**Other titles
in the series**
Easy French
Easy Greek
Easy Italian

To order any of these titles, please telephone
0870 787 1732. For further information about all
Collins books, visit our website: www.collins.co.uk